AN ARCHITECTURAL GUIDEBOOK TO THE NATIONAL PARKS
Arizona, New Mexico, Texas

AN ARCHITECTURAL GUIDEBOOK TO THE NATIONAL PARKS

Arizona, New Mexico, Texas

Harvey H. Kaiser

Gibbs Smith, Publisher
Salt Lake City

First Edition
07 06 05 04 03   5 4 3 2 1

Published by
Gibbs Smith, Publisher
P.O. Box 667
Layton, Utah 84041

Orders: (1-800) 748-5439
www.gibbs-smith.com

Edited by Jennifer Adams
Designed by J. Scott Knudsen
Printed and bound in the United States of America

Library of Congress Cataloging-in-Publication Data

Kaiser, Harvey H., 1936-
  An architectural guidebook to the National Parks :
Arizona, New
  Mexico, Texas / Harvey Kaiser.— 1st ed.
      p. cm.
Includes index.
ISBN 1-58685-068-7
  1. Architecture—West (U.S.)—Guidebooks. 2. Historic
buildings—West
(U.S.)—Guidebooks. 3. National parks and reserves—West
(U.S.)—Guidebooks. I. Title.
  NA725 .K347 2003
  720'.978—dc21
                                2002153624

CONTENTS

ACKNOWLEDGMENTS

We acknowledge the support of a grant from the Graham Foundation for the Advanced Study in the Fine Arts for this book.

This book evolved from years of appreciation and study of the historic architecture in natural settings. We owe acknowledgments to many individuals who inspired the idea, provided helpful advice and comments, and encouraged a venture that had the possibility of becoming an overwhelming task. Many miles were covered in creating this book, and many people shared information and thoughts; a casual conversation with a park ranger or hotel desk clerk sometimes led the way to a place or setting that would have been missed without their patiently offered directions or advice. An apology is offered to those who, in my oversight, are not mentioned.

The publisher of Chronicle Books generously permitted the use of material that originally appeared in *Landmarks in the Landscape*, published in 1997. Some text and photographs contained in that lengthier treatise on the historic architecture of the national parks of the West is reproduced here. The deft editing hand of Jane Taylor is again appreciated where material she touched is used once more.

At Gibbs Smith, Publisher, Suzanne Taylor led the encouragement to continue a long journey only begun across the National Park System. I owe a debt to Jennifer Adams, who coordinated editing and book production. She earns an award for a strong but gentle hand.

Without the generous contribution of time and interest of the National Park Service staff, the book would still be an unrealized ambition. In the NPS Washington office, Randall Biallas, Chief Historical Architect, and Gordon Fairchild encouraged the book's concept and permitted access to a trove of invaluable material. Gordon patiently led me through the NPS database of classified structures, doing so with tolerance for frequent questions. This research formed the backbone of the content for the book. In the Harpers Ferry Design Center, the indefatigable Tom Durant provided me with images from the NPS photo files, always with a gentle tolerance for short deadlines.

There is a special acknowledgment to Rodd Wheaton, Assistant Regional Director NPS Intermountain Region, for his frequent and rapid responses to my questions. Rodd offered invaluable information on the parks that guided selections in this book. However, the author takes full responsibility for final choices. I also appreciate the many park superintendents and park staff that commented on the draft manuscript on short notice to help make sure I got it right. Their responses caught errors and omissions and corrected my novel grammar. A special praise is due to the many park rangers and volunteers whose informative conversations and tours informed and enriched the park experience. Regrettably, their names were not recorded and they will remain unsung contributors to this book.

An acknowledgment is due to the many people who participated in the Historic American Building Survey/Historic American Engineering Record. The HABS/HAER files accessible by Internet provided historical documents as well as carefully researched and artfully drawn renditions of many historic structures in the National Park System.

Use of material from National Park Service publications is acknowledged with respect for thoroughness in research and skillful writing. Publications of the National Park Service, including administrative histories available on the Internet and Historic Structures Reports, are often primary research sources that I found paraphrased by other authors. My principal acknowledgment is to the talented and diligent National Park Service historians who created a reliable record of individual parks, events, and people that I, like other authors, found invaluable. I owe an acknowledgment for use of material by other authors built on the foundation of National Park Service research.

Finally, my gratitude to my wife, Linda, for her advice and travel companionship, her map reading skills, her fine use of language, and her patience for the commitment to continue on this journey across a marvelous country.

INTRODUCTION

The National Park System contains the scenic and historic treasures of our country. The natural beauty of the parks is profusely described in soaring phrases by outstanding writers, captured majestically in photographs and paintings, and listed and cross-tabulated in a host of travel guides. Why, then, a guidebook to architecture when the central purpose of the parks seems to be their natural resources?

Part of the answer is found in the Organic Act of 1916 founding the National Park Service, " . . . which purpose is to conserve the scenery and the natural and historic objects and the wild life therein and to provide for the enjoyment of the same in such a manner and by such means as will leave them unimpaired for the enjoyment of future generations." Because of the phrase "historic objects," many units of the National Park System are buildings, albeit often in sublime settings. In addition to recognizable national landmarks—the Statue of Liberty, Washington Monument, and Abraham Lincoln Birthplace—there is a collection of cultural resources in the National Park System that draws the visitor's attention. Presidents' homes, historic lodges and hotels, and National Park Service rustic cabins are abundant throughout the parks. Some historic structures are shadowed by interstate highways in downtown areas of the city while others are discovered after hours of driving across deserts.

Another part of the answer to "why an architectural guidebook" is that there is simply none available dedicated to that purpose. As an architect traveling the country I found myself agreeing with Wallace Stegner that "National Parks are the best idea we ever had." After standing awestruck at the first sight of the Grand Canyon and Guadalupe Mountains and exploring the natural wonders, I often silently congratulated the vision that preserved the unique "idea." It was after I turned my attention away from the main attraction and noticed buildings, not the honky-tonk or roadside tourist eyesores clustered at park entrances, but the buildings of form and materials strong enough to carry away as an image of a park that seemed to fit with the landscape. In addition to the national park great lodges there are remnants of prehistory native people, Spanish missions, and army forts commemorating important moments in our country's history.

This second book in a series of guidebooks on the historic architecture of the national park system takes the reader to parks in Arizona, New Mexico, and Texas. Within these states are landscapes of dramatic vistas across mountains, mesas, and desert vitalized by rivers and springs. A rich heritage of ruins, restored buildings, and modern structures in sublime settings offer a vibrant panorama to reward the traveler. Historic architecture in units of the national park system protect, preserve, and interpret a varied collection of structures in the vastness of the American Southwest.

Across the vast areas of these states (a reminder to the traveler of distances), millennia of settlement by native people is overlaid by other people and events that are visible in modern ruins and National Park Service facilities. The ruins of mysteriously abandoned pueblos dot the area, standing starkly on ridges, along streams and wash beds, and high in niches in cliff walls. This was a cross-roads of cultures, evidence of the relatively brief span of habitation by the Chacoan and Anasazi people. Located near water sources ranging from the free-flowing Rio Grande and Pecos River to the sandy-bottomed Chaco Wash, the prehistory parks each have a unique history and characteristics defining them as worthy of preservation as a unit of the National Park System. Several are recognized for their special character with designation as National Historic Landmarks; Chaco Culture National Historic Park is a World Heritage Site.

The Spanish influence of two-and-a-half centuries left us a rich legacy of missions—remnants of visions of treasure and saved souls. Adapting to the harshness of the arid climate, the Franciscan missionaries furthered the evolution of the Spanish Colonial style, drawing on traditions of Spain and Mexico and using locally available materials and methods of construction. Built, occupied, and then abandoned after secularization in 1824, the mission complexes are in various stages of preservation and restoration that inform us of daily life of the missionaries and native people.

This land—rich in prospects of mineral wealth below the ground, and in game, productive grazing, and farmland above the ground—attracted hunters, pioneers, traders, and settlers. The argonauts heading west crossed the region on the Santa Fe and other trails. To protect new "discoverers" of the Southwest from marauding tribes, the U.S. army came and left behind the moldering ruins of forts, solitary reminders of a romanticized era of our history in a parched landscape.

In the twentieth century, with the founding of the National Park Service in 1916, facilities to accommodate visitors to sublime settings appeared at places like the Grand Canyon and Petrified Forest National Parks and Bandelier National Monument. These structures, some worthy of National Historic Landmark designation, enrich the visitor experience.

We traveled through the area to visit the parks and consulted with national parks staff to select the parks in this book. Of the forty-eight units of the National Park System in Arizona, New Mexico, and Texas we selected twenty-one parks—eleven in Arizona, six in New Mexico, and four in Texas. Why choose some places and omit others? The author's preferences are based on architectural significance and a desire to select places of interest that illustrate how diverse cultures responded to the environment. The aim is to assist the traveler who has a curiosity about why structures appear where they do, who built them, how they were built, and insights into the history of a place marked by civilization's imprint on the landscape.

Some places in this book will involve long drives to a single remote building, such as Arizona's Pipe Spring National Monument and Hubbell Trading Post National Historic Site. Others are convenient to the metropolitan areas of Phoenix, Albuquerque, and San Antonio. Army forts were placed for strategic reasons and not the convenience of modern motorists. And the reward of reaching the Grand Canyon south or north rim and standing in awe at nature's work is enriched by the stunning work of architects Gilbert Stanley Underwood, Mary Jane Colter, and the National Park Service's talented designers. All found ways to respect the environment and merge their egos into admirable buildings that are memorable experiences.

A note to the traveler: Plan ahead for routes that will take you across many miles from park to park. There are convenient loops from Flagstaff for several parks. San Antonio's missions are close to downtown. Albuquerque has several parks nearby that are relatively short drives from the airport. Certainly, among parks not included in this guidebook, magical places like Big Bend National Park in Texas and El Morro National Monument, White Sands National Monument, and Carlsbad Caverns National Park in New Mexico should not be bypassed because they were not included here.

You should look over regional and state maps to chart overnight stays and possible restaurant stops. They may be few and far between on the drive to some parks. The National Park Service web page (www.nps.gov) is an excellent resource. It should be accessed for trip planning, including links to information on park history, travel directions, and weather information. Heed the advice of bringing water and the cautions about respecting fragile sites and privacy of National park service staff.

A note to the photographer: There are travel web pages and scenic guidebooks filled with photographs saturated with reds and oranges that enrich a structure. From my experience, these fine images are the result of early or late hours of the rising and setting sun; such results require patience and good luck in lighting conditions.

You will find park bookstores are well-stocked with publications on local history and backgrounds of people and events. We found several sources that were extremely helpful and occasionally paraphrased. Thomas Drain's *A Sense of Mission: Historic Churches of the Southwest* is a handsome and informative presentation of Spanish missions. Robert and Florence Lister's *Those Who Came Before Us* and David Grand Noble's *Ancient Ruins of the Southwest* are excellent documentation of southwestern archeology in the National Park System. Their record of the pick-and-shovel archeologists who recreated original pueblo communities will inspire your appreciation of ancient cultures.

The reader will note that there are personal observations scattered throughout the park and building descriptions. The technical descriptions of "core-and-veneer sandstone masonry walls" and documentation of building dimensions are balanced with an appreciation of a setting, events, and personalities. Sidebars highlight events and characters with brief biographies.

Visits to the parks in this guidebook should be done with frequent pauses to "feel" a place. Linger for a while on the plaza at Aztec Ruins, the naves of the Pecos and Quarai Mission churches, a bench below Montezuma Castle, and the lounge of Grand Canyon Lodge. Your personal reflections will highlight a visit to these treasures of the National Park System.

HOW TO USE THIS GUIDEBOOK

The organization of this book is by states and then by individual parks. The twenty-one parks described here—eleven in Arizona, six in New Mexico, and four in Texas—are difficult to see in a single journey. Better to plan in advance for different regions or serendipitous opportunities when combined with other travel plans.

Maps introducing each state show the general location of parks and nearby major cities. For each park there are travel directions and a brief background of the park's history as a general orientation to the significance of the historic structure(s). A web page address is useful for travel planning and park background information. Parks with multiple buildings are described in a sequence that follows a driving tour and hiking access to remote locations. An invaluable resource for full enjoyment of a park is found in the National Park Service brochures available at each site. These handsomely illustrated and well-researched publications can guide a rewarding visit. For those with a deeper interest in the structures described here, visit the Historic American Building Survey/Historic Architecture and Engineering Record (HABS/HAER) at http://lcweb2.loc.gov. The thorough research and documentation in photographs, drawings, and text by teams of technicians can be inspected and downloaded.

The season of the year and weather can limit access to some areas. Plan for weather extremes: a sudden midsummer downpour or a baking desert sun require flexibility in plans, clothing, and equipment.

Days and hours of access, parking, and disabled accessibility can be checked by Internet reference to www.nps.gov. The National Park Service web site has a page for each park that unfolds with layers of information useful to the traveler.

The nomenclature of the National Park System is useful to sort out the variety of parks in the system. The diversity of parks is reflected in the variety of titles given to them. These include such designations as national park, national preserve, national monument, national memorial, national historic site, national seashore, and national battlefield park. Although some titles are self-explanatory, others have been used in many different ways. For example, the title "national monument" has been given to natural reservations, historic military fortifications, prehistoric ruins, fossil sites, and the Statue of Liberty.

In recent years, both Congress and the National Park Service have attempted to simplify the nomenclature and establish basic criteria for use of the different titles and additions to the National Park System. The nation's profound interest in protecting the natural and cultural resources has a suitable framework for protection that will undoubtedly expand the future number of parks. The following are definitions of the most common titles:

National Lakeshores and Seashores

Preserved shoreline areas and offshore islands, with a focus on preservation of natural values while at the same time providing water-oriented recreation.

National Historic Sites and National Historic Parks

Parks designated as national historic sites preserve places and commemorate persons, events, and activities important in the nation's history. National historical parks are commonly areas of greater physical extent and complexity than national historic sites.

National Memorial

Parks that are primarily commemorative. They need not be sites or structures historically associated with their subjects. For example, the home of Abraham Lincoln in Springfield, Illinois, is a national historic site, but the Lincoln Memorial in the District of Columbia is a national memorial.

National Monument

A national monument, usually smaller than a national park and lacking its diversity of attractions, is intended to preserve at least one nationally significant resource.

National Military Park, National Battlefield Park, National Battlefield Site, and National Battlefield

Areas associated with American military history.

National Park

Generally, national parks are areas containing a variety of resources protected by large land or water areas.

National Parkways

Parks that include ribbons of land flanking roadways and offer an opportunity for driving through areas of scenic interest.

National Recreation Areas

Parks with lands and waters set aside for recreational use now include major areas in urban centers. There are also national recreation areas outside the National Park System that are administered by the National Forest Service, U.S. Department of Agriculture.

National Rivers and Wild and Scenic Rivers

Parks that preserve ribbons of land bordering on free-flowing streams that have not been dammed, channeled, or otherwise altered. Besides preserving rivers in their natural states, these areas provide opportunities for outdoor activities.

National Scenic Trails

Generally, long-distance footpaths winding through areas of natural beauty.

Related Areas

Besides the National Park System, four groups of areas exist—Affiliated Areas, National Heritage areas, the Wild and Scenic Rivers System, and the National Trails System—that are closely linked in importance and purpose to those areas managed by the National Park Service. Not all these areas are units of the National Park System, yet they preserve important segments of the nation's heritage.

ARIZONA

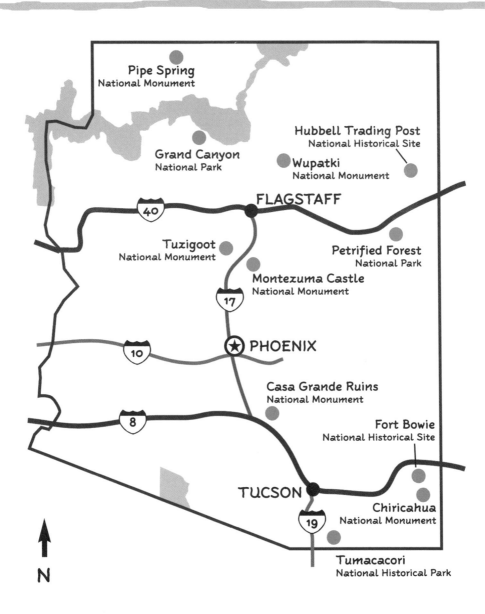

Pipe Spring
National Monument

Hubbell Trading Post
National Historical Site

Grand Canyon
National Park

Wupatki
National Monument

40 FLAGSTAFF

Tuzigoot
National Monument

Petrified Forest
National Park

Montezuma Castle
National Monument

17

10   ★ PHOENIX

Casa Grande Ruins
National Monument

Fort Bowie
National Historical Site

8

TUCSON

Chiricahua
National Monument

19

N

Tumacacori
National Historical Park

CASA GRANDE RUINS

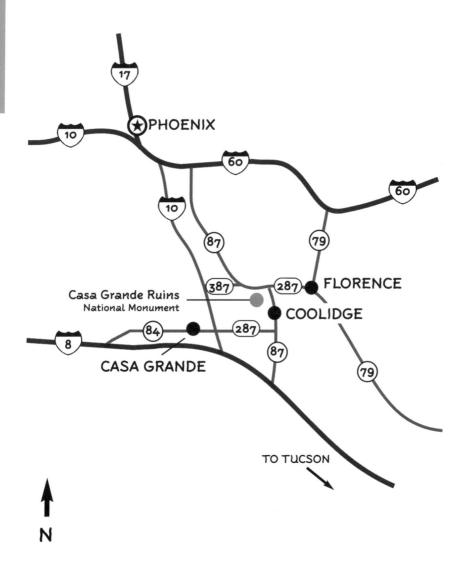

1

Casa Grande Ruins
National Monument

Coolidge, Pinal County, Arizona
www.nps.gov/cagr

Casa Grande Ruins National Monument is in southern Arizona, halfway between Phoenix and Tucson. Take I-10 south from Phoenix to exit 185, then go east on Highway 287 and 87 for 14 miles. The monument is one mile north of Coolidge.

> ". . . the Casa Grande is a four story building, as large as a castle and equal to the largest church in these lands of Sonora. Close to this Casa Grande there are thirteen smaller houses, somewhat more dilapidated, and the ruins of many others, which make it evident that in ancient times there had been a city here."
>
> *Kino's Historical Memoir of Pimeria Alta: A Contemporary*
> *Account of the Beginnings of California, Sonora, and Arizona,*
> Father Eusebio Francisco Kino (published
> originally in 1708, translated in 1919)

Casa Grande Ruins National Monument preserves and interprets the Classic Period of the Hohokam culture. The Hohokam (Piman for "those who have gone") is thought to be related to the present-day Pima. The monument's main feature is the Great House (*Casa Grande* in Spanish), surrounded by the remains of smaller buildings and a compound wall constructed in the early 1200s and abandoned by the mid-1400s. The curved adobe walls at the monument entrance and visitor center are a prelude to the massive, four-story Great House standing under its idiosyncratic protective roof on four inwardly canted columns. Recognized for its significance as a prehistoric ruin, the monument was the first archeological site to be preserved (1892) and is the fifth oldest unit in the National Park system. The 472-acre site was redesignated a national monument in 1918.

DISCOVERY AND PRESERVATION

At the settlement site beginning around A.D. 200 to 500, the Hohokam prospered as desert farmers at Casa Grande through a sophisticated irrigation system of canals from the Gila River two miles north. By A.D. 1300, the settlement was the center of cultivated fields, with a village of Pueblo-like compounds surrounding a ballcourt and community plaza. Though the Great House was in use for only several generations of the Classic Period (A.D. 100 to 1450), it was part of a larger settlement complex. Sometime between 1355 and 1450 a slow societal collapse occurred, and the Hohokam culture disappeared. Archeologists speculate on causes of the disappearance of the Hohokam: failure of the irrigation system; soil depletion from extensive irrigation, along with climatic changes and flooding; raiding by neighboring tribes; or disease. Whatever the reasons, the desert reclaimed the land and erosion began to melt the once-magnificent Great House back into the sand.

Father Eusebio Francisco Kino, a Jesuit missionary, was the first European to visit the Casa Grande ruins. In 1694, he reached the ruins, said a mass within its towering walls, and wrote an account in his journal, describing it as a four-story *casa grande* as large as a castle or any other church then in Sonora. Kino returned to Casa Grande several times, and accompanying soldiers provided even more details of the settlement and its canals.

The ruins were a landmark for eighteenth- and nineteenth-century explorers, trappers, soldiers, settlers, and tourists who recorded their impressions. The Great House measured approximately fifty-eight feet by forty-three feet, and its alignment was almost, but not quite, in line with the cardinal points. By 1880, a Southern Pacific Railroad station twenty miles away connected stage tours to the ruins. The looting and vandalism of the site, along with the continued erosion of the structures, raised national interest in preservation. Photographs from 1878, compared to sketches from the 1840s, show that corners at the northeast and southeast had fallen away. Archeological excavations starting in the 1880s recorded the toll of time and tourists on the ruins. In 1890, Cosmos Mindeleff visited the ruins and reported that tourists had "torn out and carried away every lintel and every particle of visible wood in the building." Defaced by inscriptions and with a weakening south wall, the erosion at the base of the walls from capillary action upward from the ground represented the greatest danger to the Great House.

Above: Visitor center and Great House ruins.
Right: An 1864 drawing of the Great House, from J.
Ross Browne's Adventure in the Apache Country.

Mindeleff's report triggered the movement to stabilize and protect the ruins, a
movement that raised arguments about
restoration versus stabilization or protection. In 1891, the Great House base was
underpinned with brick and faced with concrete, as seen today. It was then that
the debate emerged about providing a protective covering for the Great House.
The idea was at first dismissed by Mindeleff and later by Frank Pinkley, the first
custodian of the Reserve, as something that would destroy the picturesqueness
of the ruins. By 1903, however, a framework of ten-by-ten-inch redwood posts
with bracing struts, anchoring cables, and a corrugated iron roof was in place. By

Frank ◆———— "Boss" ————◆ Pinkley

J. Frank "Boss" Pinkley (1891–1940)

Arriving in Phoenix from his home in Missouri in September 1900 to recuperate from a mild case of tuberculosis, nineteen-year-old Frank Pinkley stayed longer than a scheduled six months and began an adventure that would last a lifetime. Little more than a year after his arrival in Arizona, Pinkley eagerly accepted the offer of a government position as caretaker of a prehistoric ruin in the desert of the Gila River Valley. He brought his new bride, Edna Townsley, to live in a frame-sided tent pitched in a mesquite grove in the shadow of the Great House. He dug his own well, wrote his reports to the General Land Office at a desk he had made, and later, with his own funds, built an adobe house at the ruins. When Casa Grande was designated a national monument in 1918, the National Park Service offered Pinkley the job of resident custodian, but there was a catch: he would also be expected to take charge of Tumacacori National Monument and several others. In 1924, the Southwestern National Monuments Office was formed, and Pinkley was designated superintendent in charge of fourteen monuments.

Pinkley was a tireless promoter of Casa Grande and other southwestern monuments, although continually frustrated that funding lagged behind the need to protect them from vandalism and disintegration. Frequently, he paid for his own travel or went without his annual salary to provide much-needed repairs. At the time of his death in 1940, Pinkley administered twenty-seven national monuments in four states.

"The Boss," as Pinkley was affectionately known to his cohorts and employees, left a singular legacy. "Ruminations from The Boss" was a collection of topical, often humorous essays by Pinkley that punctuated the monthly reports compiled by his staff. In his Ruminations, Pinkley revealed an uncanny ability to explain, instruct, and cajole in a fatherly way. In 1932, Pinkley wrote prophetically, "In all this rushing and roaring around and growing into a bigger organization, let us watch carefully that the Park Service spirit, the spirit of service, doesn't evaporate."

the mid-1920s, the roof's deterioration prompted study of a replacement. In 1928, Frederick Law Olmsted Jr., acting in an advisory capacity to the National Park Service, sketched a design for a new roof. Funds became available in 1932, and the Park Service proceeded with construction of a hip roof on a steel frame, incorporating Olmsted's distinctive leaning posts and curved

Steel and concrete canopy erected in 1932 to protect the Great House.

outer truss members. Guy wires were omitted and a copper-louvered ventilator was placed at the roof's apex to withstand upward wind pressure.

The Great House

Casa Grande builders found construction material in the soil below their feet: caliche, a naturally occuring concrete-like mixture of sand, clay, and calcium carbonate (limestone). It took three thousand tons to construct the Great House. Caliche mud was piled in successive courses to form walls four feet thick at the base tapering to two feet thick at the top, in four stories each thirty to forty-five feet high. An estimated 640 beams of ponderosa pine, juniper, mesquite, and fir trees were carried or floated down the Gila River approximately 50 miles or more to the village. Anchored in the walls, the timbers formed ceiling or

A diagram of the known portions of the walled compound with the Great House highlighted. Other areas of the compound are unexcavated.

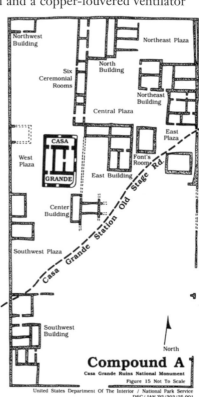

Northwest Building

Northeast Plaza

Six Ceremonial Rooms

North Building

Northeast Building

Central Plaza

West Plaza

CASA GRANDE

East Plaza

Font's Room

East Building

Center Building

Casa Grande Station Old Stage Rd.

Southwest Plaza

Southwest Building

North

Compound A

Casa Grande Ruins National Monument

Figure 15 Not To Scale

United States Department Of The Interior / National Park Service
DSC/JAN '92/303/25.001

floor supports. A lattice of saguaro ribs was placed perpendicular across the beams, covered with bundles of reeds, and topped with a final layer of caliche mud.

Caliche mud was mixed to a thick consistency in holes in the ground, carried to the walls, and then placed in courses about twenty-six inches high without internal reinforcing. Evidence of the hand-forming process is visible in the handprints, which can still be seen in the walls. Built on five feet of fill, the present height of the house closely approximates the original height of four stories. The first story was purposefully filled in during construction; the second and third stories each had five rooms; a single room or tower comprised the fourth floor; and a low parapet may have surrounded the uppermost floor levels. The fourth-story room has a tunnel-like opening in one wall that aligns with the setting sun at summer solstice.

The southwest corner of the walled compound to the left of the sheltered Great House.

Efforts to stabilize the moisture-susceptible caliche mud began in the 1890s when exposed walls were capped with concrete, and later, endless attempts to find a satisfactory chemical preservative were made. Drainage work around the base walls helped solve some of the moisture problem. Ironically, the most effective wall preservation technique, one probably advocated in 1902, was a light coating of caliche mud. The "magic formula" now in use is called Amended Mud, a mixture of a commercial product and caliche mixed with sand, first tested in 1972. Applied every two years by whisk broom, a coating of this brownish-colored substance allows the capillary moisture in the walls to evaporate.

The function of Casa Grande remains an enigma to this day. Without written record of the desert people, speculation has been cast about on the use of the Great House as a defensive watch tower, an observation point for the life-sustaining irrigation canal to the north, a corn storehouse, and a religious center. Archeoastronomers—those who apply the study of celestial events at archeological sites—speculate that the Great House's orientation to the cardinal points and upper-room oval, circular, and rectangular sun or calendar holes were placed for special purposes. Knowing the changing positions of celestial objects guided ceremonial cycles and planting and harvesting.

National Park Service Buildings

The National Park Service buildings at the Monument evolved from Frank Pinkley's house and a museum, refined by a 1928 master plan supervised by Thomas Vint from the Park Service's San Francisco field headquarters. In 1932, construction was completed on a new museum/administration structure and residences for Pinkley and an assistant; the older 1926 museum was converted to a residence. The house was designed in a modified Pueblo architectural style; dirt for the adobe brick came from the 1906–7 excavations of Compound A.

Pueblo-style visitor center and museum built in 1932.

The National Park Service publication *Park and Recreation Structures* (1938) highly commended the partially completed Administration Building design:

> Adobe, in gesture to tradition, and low, in keeping with the surrounding expanse of level terrain, this building is definitely and excellently custom-tailored to the Southwest. It houses various facilities that have legitimate function as phases of park administration and conveys impressively a feeling of organized administrative authority. The architectural style is related to that of the entranceway and entrance sign of this same park.

Today's visitor center was conceived as a hollow square around an open courtyard, but insufficient funds resulted in completion of only the front part of the square. In 1964, work resumed, and exhibit space was added to create the courtyard, with native plants, a new entrance, and a covered porch along the building's north side.

Additional areas outside the ruins are visible from the observation deck in the picnic area. Although the ruins are open in daylight hours for self-guided tours, an orientation and tour conducted by a Park Service Ranger begins in the interpretive ramada and is recommended for the start of a journey back in time to the enigmatic Great House of the Hohokam.

CHIRICAHUA

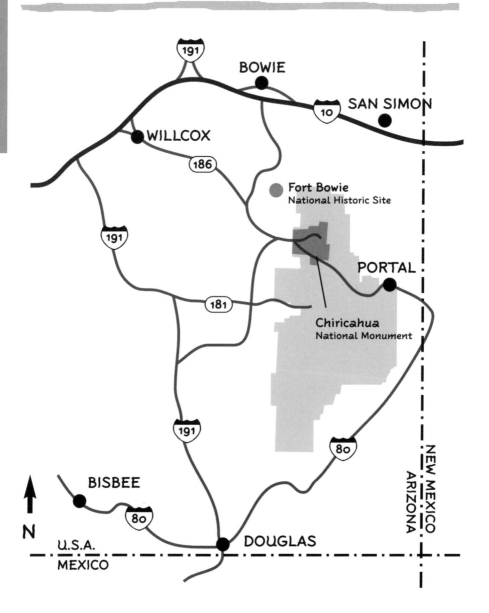

2

Chiricahua
National Monument

Near Willcox, Cochise County, Arizona
www.nps.gov/chir

The monument is in the southeast corner of Arizona, 70 miles east of Tucson on I-10. Take exit 340 at Willcox, then go southeast on Route 186 for 35 miles. At Route 181 go east approximately 4 miles to the visitor center.

"... forty-five hundred acres of varicolored monoliths carved by erosion and grotesque figures that seem to march along the mountainside like invaders from some fantastic region."

Arizona: A Guide to the Youngest State,
American Guide Series, Writer's Program,
Works Progress Administration, 1940

Deep into the southeast corner of Arizona—fifteen miles west of New Mexico, fifty miles north of the Mexican border, and twenty miles from Fort Bowie National Historic Site—is the landscape of the Turkey Creek caldera. Formed by a massive volcanic eruption twenty-seven million years ago, two thousand feet of ash and pumice fused into a rock called rhyolite tuff and eventually eroded into towering spires, pinnacles, and balanced rocks weighing hundreds of tons that perch delicately on small pedestals. Here, at the intersection of the Chihuahuan and Sonoran deserts, the southern Rocky Mountains, and the northern Sierra Madre of Mexico, is a place of diverse wildlife and plants. Called the "Land of the Standing-Up Rocks" by Chiricahua Apaches and later the "Wonderland of Rocks" by pioneers, twelve thousand acres of this land was set aside as Chiricahua National Monument in 1924 and transferred from the Forest Service to the National Park Service in 1933. Of historic interest are the homesteads of Faraway Ranch, a restored working cattle ranch and later a guest ranch, and the Stafford Cabin.

HOMESTEADERS

The Chiricahua Mountains were the homeland of the Chiricahua Apaches. Led by Cochise and Geronimo, the Apaches launched attacks from these mountains against the tide of pioneers that began in 1866. The Apache resistance slowed but did not stop settlement of the area, and Geronimo's band surrendered in 1886. Remains of the tent camp and stone monument markers of a 10th Cavalry troop (Buffalo Soldiers), which were part of the campaign against Geronimo's Chiricahua Apaches in 1885 and 1886, have been discovered in the National Monument. With Geronimo's surrender and his removal to the distant reservation of Fort Sill, Oklahoma, a new way of life took over.

Stafford Cabin

Jay Hugh Stafford arrived in 1880 and built one of the first homestead dwellings in the Chiricahua Mountains vicinity. The Stafford Cabin illustrates the techniques and building materials used in one of the oldest surviving log cabins in the region. Built of logs from adjacent forests, the original two-room cabin (approximately fifteen by twenty-eight feet, with later shed and garage additions) has a ridge roof with exposed log purlins and wood-plank ceiling. The simple interiors had pine flooring and a rhyolite fieldstone chimney in the living room. The site surrounding the cabin has evidence of Stafford's early agricultural efforts: an orchard of fruit trees and an irrigation system. After around 1919, the Stafford Cabin was remodeled as a guest cabin for the neighboring Faraway Ranch, a commercial guest ranch operated by Lillian and Ed Riggs.

Faraway Ranch

A Swedish emigrant couple, Neil Erickson and his wife Emma, came to homestead in Bonita Canyon soon after Stafford did. In 1886, then–army sergeant Erickson came upon the canyon while he was pursuing a horse stolen from Col. Hughes Safford by an Apache named Massai. The couple built a home in the canyon, farmed the land, and raised a family. By 1917, one of the Ericksons' daughters, Lillian, and her husband Ed Riggs had turned the homestead into a guest ranch. Lillian, the strong-willed "Lady Boss," named the ranch Faraway Ranch, because it was so "godawful far away from everything." Together, she and Ed explored the land, built trails, and took guests on horseback trips. They showed photographs of the rock formations at county fairs and chambers of commerce meetings, and promoted the idea of making Chiricahua a national park. Their efforts eventually helped it gain its current status as a national monument in 1924.

Ed and Lillian Riggs expanded Faraway Ranch into one of the leading guest

Chiricahua National Monument balanced rock formations are carved out of volcanic ash hardened into rhyolite rock by erosion forces of water, wind, and ice.

ranches in southeastern Arizona. The Erickson house was the center of activities, and the ranch eventually grew to include guest cottages and a swimming pool. Operated by the couple until Ed's death in 1950 and by Lillian alone until the early 1970s, the National Park Service acquired the property in separate purchases in 1972 and 1978. Listed on the National Register of Historic Places, the ranch includes the Ericksons' house and cottages. The house is restored with original furnishings to reflect the 1950s historic period, when it achieved its height of success as a guest ranch.

Erickson, a self-taught carpenter, erected the ranch house in three major stages. The resulting two-story mixture of adobe, wood framing, exterior stucco, and shingle roof stands in a grove on the canyon's floor. The dining room fireplace rocks were originally part of a monument to James A. Garfield built by the Buffalo Soldiers stationed in Bonita Canyon. The Buffalo Soldiers who built the monument to honor Garfield, a well-liked commander of black troops in the Civil War, inscribed the rocks. Tours of the main house at Faraway Ranch are conducted daily.

FORT BOWIE

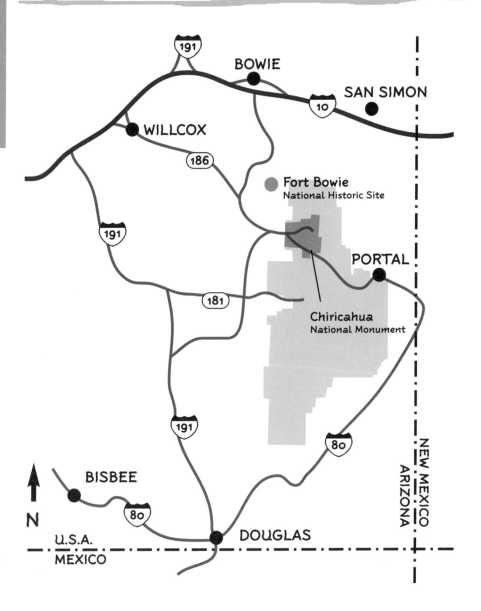

3

Fort Bowie
National Historic Site

Near Willcox and Bowie, Cochise County, Arizona
www.nps.gov/fobo

Access to the Fort Bowie National Historic Site in southeast Arizona is from I-10. From the west, take exit 340 at Willcox, go 25 miles on Highway 186 to the Fort Bowie turnoff, then north on the Apache Pass Road for about 9 miles to the Fort Bowie trailhead. From the east, take exit 366 at Bowie, then go 12 miles south on the gravel to the trailhead. The fort is reached by following a rugged 1-1/2-mile sand-and-gravel trail leading to the trailhead.

> ". . . weathered ruins, which stand like ghostly sentinels guarding the memory of a turbulent past."
>
> *The Guide to the National Parks of the Southwest,*
> Southwest Parks and Museum Association (2001)

Fort Bowie is located near the summit of Apache Pass, between the Chiricahua and Dos Cabezas Mountains in southeastern Arizona. For centuries, Apache Pass was an important crossing point due to the natural springs there. Troops stationed at Fort Bowie were involved in some of the most hard-fought battles between soldiers and Indians in the American Southwest from 1861 to 1886, including battles with Apache leaders Cochise and Geronimo. The 1,000-acre site was authorized in 1964 and established as a National Historic Site in 1972.

When visiting the site, gather your memories of all the great westerns featuring the Apache Wars, tuck a copy of Paul Horgan's *A Distant Trumpet* in your backpack along with water, and take the trail 1-1/2 miles along the old military road to experience the place. Here, Apache leaders and their followers fought long and hard for their homeland. This is where operations centered against the

Chiricahua Apaches under Mangas Coloradas, Cochise, and Geronimo in battles for more than twenty-five years. It is all ruins now—the Butterfield Overland Mail stage station, the post cemetery, Apache Spring, the site of the first Fort Bowie from 1862, and from 1869 fragments of the second fort's ochre-colored eroding adobe walls.

No battles were fought at Fort Bowie; the climate and terrain favored the Indians, skilled in guerilla warfare, where the odds were overwhelmingly in their favor. For the soldiers stationed here, the garrison life consisted chiefly of tedium—endless marches under the desert sun and lonely barracks life—and rare chances to face the elusive Apaches. With few visible remains on the site other than the stabilized walls, your experience is to drift back in time to a tumultuous piece of American legend: the Apache Wars.

For several hundred years, this region was home to the nomadic Chiricahua Apaches who often raided pueblos, explorers, and settlers indiscriminately for food. Spaniards traveling through Apache Pass were ambushed so frequently they called it *Puerto del Dado* (Pass of Death). Two years after the Gadsden Purchase in 1854, a military route was laid out through the Pass, taking advantage of a year-round spring. In 1858, John Butterfield inaugurated semiweekly mail service to California and built a watering station for Butterfield Overland Mail at Apache Springs. The first Fort Bowie was established in 1862, and replaced in 1869 by a larger fort built nearby. Both were made primarily of adobe. The post survived until 1894.

Travelers and mail stages moved through the area largely unhindered until the Bascom Affair in April 1861. A raid by a band of Apaches on a nearby ranch was wrongly attributed to Cochise and his Chiricahuas. Lt. George N. Bascom and fifty-four men pursued the Apache leader and, in a camp a mile from the fort, maneuvered Cochise into his tent. Outraged at the accusation, Cochise is reputed to have slashed his way through the tent wall, escaping the soldiers cordoned outside. But some of his companions were captured and hanged. The volatile situation rapidly escalated between Cochise's warriors and the army troops, with hostages taken and killed by the Indians, prisoners taken by the military, and Butterfield stagecoaches and freight caravans attacked by the Indians. This bloody encounter, which came to be called the Bascom Affair, opened up a long period of warfare between the Chiricahua Apaches and the settlers, lasting until the surrender of Geronimo in 1886 and the banishment of the Chiricahuas first to Florida, next to Alabama, and finally to Fort Sill, Oklahoma.

The year following the dramatic escape by Cochise and the ensuing hostilities, Union troops withdrew from the area to fight in the Civil War. This opened up New Mexico and Arizona to Confederate invasion. The Apaches bloodied Texans that arrived in the summer of 1861 until a troop of California Volunteer Infantry

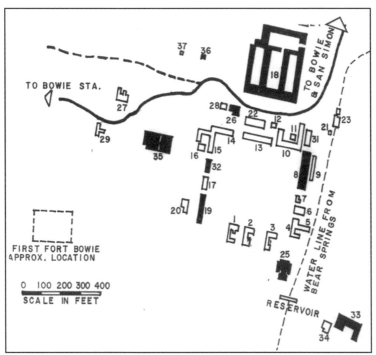

Fort Bowie site plan in the 1890s. Corrals (#18) are north of the parade grounds faced by officers quarters (#1 through #6), barracks (#1 and #9), and schoolhouse (#32). The commanding officers quarters (#25), post trader-sutler's store (#35), and new hospital (#33) are outside the parade ground grouping.

arrived under the command of Maj. T. A. Coult to drive out the Confederates. On July 15–16, 1862, five hundred Chiricahuas and Gilas, led by Cochise and Coloradas Mangas, ambushed the volunteers. The volunteer infantry was saved by artillery fired on the braves, however the Battle of Apache Pass persuaded Brig. Gen. James H. Carleton to order Fort Bowie built to protect both the pass and Apache Spring. Soldiers from Company G, 5th California Infantry began its construction on July 28, 1862, on a hill overlooking the spring. It was named for the regiment's commanding officer, Col. George Washington Bowie.

Completed in less than three weeks, the first Fort Bowie of thirteen tents surrounded by irregular stone breastworks was quickly constructed at key positions on top of the hill. As winter approached, the tents were replaced by crude adobe, stone, and log quarters, which one officer called "mere hovels . . . through which rain passes very much as it would through a sieve." A second and less primitive Fort Bowie was started in 1868 on a plateau about three hundred yards southeast of the original.

California and New Mexico volunteers guarded the pass during the Civil War years, and were replaced by regular U.S. troops in 1866. Although the garrison held three hundred soldiers at its peak in 1886, the average numbered around one hundred.

An 1871 peace treaty creating a 3,000-acre reservation taking in the Chiricahua Mountains interrupted the long saga of the Chiricahua Apache's clashes with the settlers and soldiers. Dissatisfied with agricultural reservation life, tensions among the Apaches mounted after Cochise's death in 1874. Relocated to San Carlos Reservation one hundred miles to the north, renegades led by Geronimo escaped and resumed raids on settlers along the border. Units from Fort Bowie under the leadership of Gen. Nelson A. Miles pursued 134 Chiricahuas led by Geronimo into Mexico. Geronimo's final surrender in September 1886 at Skelton Canyon, Arizona, brought an end to the long and bitter Apache Wars. Geronimo and his followers were brought back to Fort Bowie, assembled on the parade ground, and taken by wagons to the railroad for the long journey to exile in Florida.

Geronimo's surrender ended both the Apache Wars and Fort Bowie's usefulness as a military installation. The fort, however, remained an active post for another eight years. It was finally closed on October 17, 1894, when the last troops were withdrawn.

Fort Bowie was a typical southwestern frontier army post, much like the fictional Fort Delivery in Horgan's *A Distant Trumpet*. Adobe and wood barracks, a row of officers' quarters, storehouses, a schoolhouse, and a hospital soon occupied the four sides of the parade ground. Corrals and stables, a post trader's store, guardhouse, ice machine house, mess, and bakery ringed the parade ground buildings. Occupied in 1869, more buildings were added over the years, including a new hospital and an ornate two-story, wood-frame, Victorian-style house, erected in 1884 for the commanding officer. Nearly forty buildings were eventually constructed at the second fort: twenty-nine were of adobe, eight were frame, and one—the magazine—was constructed of stone. Officers' quarters and barracks had long wooden porches facing the parade ground.

Today Fort Bowie consists of the stone foundations of both forts, and some adobe wall fragments of the second fort. A flagpole marks the center of the parade ground. The Butterfield Overland Mail Stage Station, abandoned in 1861 when service was discontinued on the eve of the Civil War, is visible in stone foundation ruins.

After the forts' abandonment by the army, the buildings became "recycling centers" for new, private owners and surrounding communities. Virtually all reusable building materials were stripped and carted away, exposing the adobe

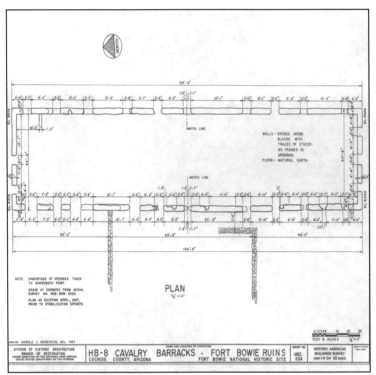

The cavalry barracks floor plan. The original structure, approximately 155 feet by 35 feet, is of adobe brick covered by stucco, with a dirt floor and a wood frame hip roof.

and foundations to the elements. A sturdy material when protected from rain and snow, adobe can last for centuries. Left unsheltered, however, it will melt back into the earth. Preservation and stabilization of Fort Bowie's adobe fragments is typical of southwest forts and other adobe National Park Service buildings.

For decades, the National Park Service has followed a policy of preserving ruins for interpretation of a park. The efforts of preserving adobe structures by using the best strategies and technologies of the day have resulted in sites being uncovered and buried; sprayed with chemicals; and capped, uncapped, mudded, plastered, and wrapped; and rebuilt, augmented, reinforced, braced, propped, and reroofed. With each change in treatment, more of the historic adobe was lost. Today, reinforcing is done very conservatively to stabilize standing building fragments. The use of chemical preservatives on adobe has been replaced by the use of more compatible materials—unamended mud shelter coats and adobe.

GRAND CANYON

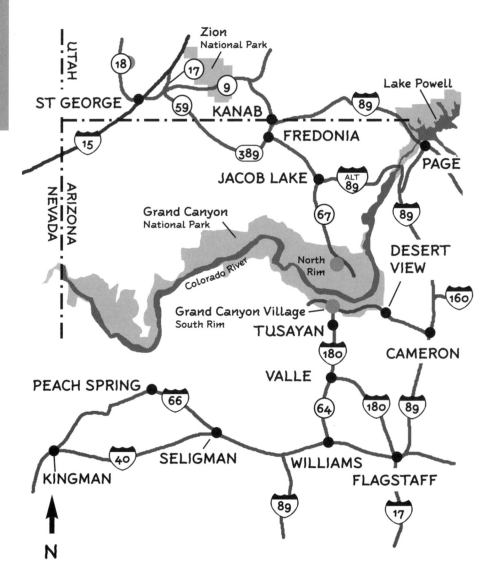

4

Grand Canyon
National Park

Grand Canyon's 277 miles along the Colorado River is north of Williams and Flagstaff in Coconino County, Arizona.
www.nps.gov/grca

Grand Canyon National Park's architectural features can be found at Grand Canyon Village on the South Rim, 60 miles north of I-40 at Williams via Highway 64, and 80 miles northwest of Flagstaff via U.S. 180; the North Rim is 41 miles south of Jacob Lake.

"Good God, something happened here."

Texas cowboy who happened upon the Grand Canyon

No matter how well prepared by photographs or descriptions, the first-time visitor to the Grand Canyon is always awestruck. The long drive to the North or South Rim, heightens the sense of disbelief; nothing prepares one for the incredible size or dramatic forms of this color-saturated canyon. From the rim down through the depths of the gorge, almost two billion years of geological history unfold. Layers of rock are visible from a vantage place matched nowhere else as deep into the earth's crust and the history of the planet's evolution.

CREATING A NATIONAL PARK

For centuries writers have tried to describe the spectacular panorama, which stretches for miles to the horizon. John Muir wrote:

GRAND CANYON VILLAGE

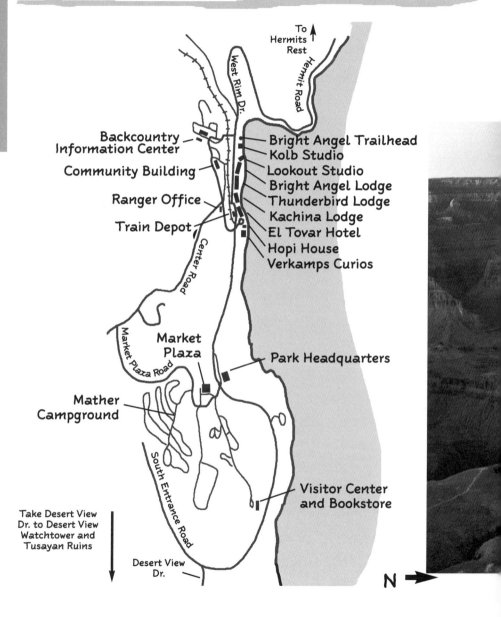

To
Hermits
Rest

Hermit Road

West Rim Dr.

Backcountry
Information Center

Community Building

Ranger Office

Train Depot

Bright Angel Trailhead
Kolb Studio
Lookout Studio
Bright Angel Lodge
Thunderbird Lodge
Kachina Lodge
El Tovar Hotel
Hopi House
Verkamps Curios

Center Road

Market Plaza Road

Market
Plaza

Park Headquarters

Mather
Campground

South Entrance Road

Take Desert View
Dr. to Desert View
Watchtower and
Tusayan Ruins

Visitor Center
and Bookstore

Desert View
Dr.

N →

Wildness so Godful, cosmic, primeval, bestows a new sense of earth's beauty and size. . . . No matter how far you have wandered hitherto, or how many famous gorges and valleys you have seen, this one, the Grand Canyon of the Colorado, will seem as novel to you, as unearthly in the color and grandeur and quantity of its architecture, as if you had found it after death, on some other star; so incomparably lovely and grand and supreme, it is above all the other canyons in our fire-molded, earthquake-shaken, rain-washed, river- and glacier-sculptured world.

John Muir described this setting in architectural terms: "Nature's grandest buildings . . . [with] endless variety of style and architecture."

John Wesley Powell described it this way: "It has infinite variety, and no part is ever duplicated. . . . By a year's toil a concept of sublimity can be obtained never again to be equaled on the hither side of Paradise."

The canyon as seen by trappers, traders, and Spanish missionaries was generally considered a terrible place, almost unworthy of mention. Part of Coronado's expedition entered the region in 1540, and the captain in command reported official dismay at the unbridgeable barrier posed by the chasm. Lt. Joseph C. Ives, exploring the lower Colorado River by steamboat in 1857, described its beauty but was pessimistic about its future usefulness. He declared, "The region, is of course, altogether valueless. . . . Ours has been the first, and will doubtless be the last, party of whites to visit this profitless locality." Ives was a poor historian and a worse prophet.

As a result of his visit to the Grand Canyon of the Colorado in the late 1890s, John Muir became an advocate for its being designated a national park. His journey to the rim of the canyon entailed a seventy-five-mile hike from the Atchison, Topeka, and Santa Fe Railroad stop at Flagstaff, Arizona. He marveled at the scene:

> After riding through these pleasure-grounds, the San Francisco and other mountains, abounding in flowery park-like openings and smooth shallow valleys with long vistas which in fineness and finish and arrangement suggest the work of a consummate landscape artist, watching all the way, you come to the most tremendous canyon in the world.

Two decades earlier, John Wesley Powell set forth on one of the greatest exploratory feats in western history. At noon on May 24, 1869, he and his team of nine men pushed off in four boats at Green River, Wyoming and began their 1,000-mile journey to the unexplored canyon and onto the confluence of the Virgin River. On August 17, they had turned from the Little Colorado into the Grand Canyon. In his journal from the expedition, *The Exploration of the Colorado River and Its Canyons*, Powell recorded his epic impressions:

> We have an unknown distance yet to run and an unknown river yet to explore. What falls there are we know not; what rocks beset the channel, we know not; what walls rise above the river, we know not. Ah, well! we may conjecture many things. The men talk as cheerfully as ever; jests are bandied about freely this morning; but to me the cheer is somber and the jests ghastly.

Powell's feats were widely broadcast through his published accounts. Subsequent expeditions by Powell and others generated guarded optimism about the potential value of tourism in the region. As artist Thomas Moran and writers Clarence Dutton and John Van Dyke extolled the beauties of the canyon, national attitudes began to change; the possibility for enjoyment replaced the potential for utility.

By the turn of the century, hotels had been built, tourist tent camps were in place, and several aerial tramways spanned the river banks in the bottom of the canyon. An eleven-hour stagecoach ride was soon replaced by a rail line. Travel increased dramatically when a spur of the Santa Fe Railway from Williams, Arizona, to the South Rim was completed in 1901. Three years later, the railway company built El Tovar Hotel. Twenty years later, the Union Pacific Railroad improved access to the North Rim and Grand Canyon Lodge via their 5-day motorcoach Loop Tour from Cedar City, Utah.

Grand Canyon Lodge in 1936. It was rebuilt after a devastating fire in 1932 destroyed the lodge and several adjacent cabins.

As a senator from Indiana, Benjamin Harrison introduced a bill that would have secured the Grand Canyon as a national park. The bill was defeated, but in 1893, as president, he signed legislation to establish Grand Canyon Forest Preserve. President Theodore Roosevelt eventually succeeded in seeing a transfer to national monument status in 1908, and an act of Congress established Grand Canyon National Park in 1919.

The architects and designers working for the railroads and the National Park Service created architectural legacies of outstanding sensitivity in the park. Many noted in the following pages as NHL are National Historic Landmark structures. The North and South Rims—separated by only ten air miles but a circuitous 215 miles by highway—are distinctly different places. The South Rim, closer to population centers, was developed first, and the Santa Fe Railway offered direct service to El Tovar Hotel. The 1923 expansion to Cedar City, Utah, by the Union Pacific Railroad opened the North Rim, with accommodations at Grand Canyon Lodge.

In many ways, the ecologically different North Rim is more attractive than the South Rim; it is about twelve hundred feet higher in elevation, cooler, has nearby forests and meadows, and far fewer visitors. The road south from Utah passes through the aspen and pine forests of the Kaibab Plateau; the San Francisco Peaks near Flagstaff can be seen seventy miles to the south and the red mountains and plateaus of Utah to the north. Cut off from the rest of Arizona by the canyon itself, the North Rim enjoys a mere 450 thousand tourists a year, compared to the South Rim's four to five million.

SOUTH RIM

The architectural attractions of the South Rim cover thirty-two miles along Desert View Drive and Hermit Road. At the center are Grand Canyon Village (NHL), the Santa Fe Railway depot (NHL), and El Tovar Hotel (NHL). Mary Jane Colter, an architect for the Fred Harvey Company, designed Hopi House (NHL), Lookout Studio (NHL), and Bright Angel Lodge (NHL). The National Park Service built the Operations Building (NHL) and Power House (NHL), excellent examples of the emerging Rustic style. Hermit Road ends at Hermits Rest (NHL). The Desert View Watchtower (NHL) and Tusayan Museum, three miles to the east of the Watchtower, are on East Rim Drive.

Grand Canyon Depot

The Santa Fe Railway in 1909 began construction of a railway depot that would be an appropriately rustic gateway to welcome travelers to El Tovar Hotel. The railroad was promoting the Grand Canyon as a destination resort and wanted visitors to the luxurious El Tovar to be impressed the moment they stepped off the train. The words "Grand Canyon" in copper letters on the gable facing the tracks and a "Santa Fe" logo centered near the ridge greeted travelers. The last passenger train pulled out of the station in 1968, and the freight office closed a year later, but in 1989 the line was reopened from

Williams to the canyon, restoring the steam locomotives that recall the early days of travel to the rim.

The depot was designed as a straightforward, functional solution to the demands of handling large volumes of passengers and freight. The first floor of the main building contained a waiting room, ticket office, baggage room, and other public spaces. An upper floor provided the station agent's apartment. A projecting, one-story log entrance porch sheltered by a gabled roof is centered on the two-story mass. The two-bay, log-column-supported waiting platform extends a lowered ridgeline from the main structure.

El Tovar Hotel

During the fierce competition for railroad customers at the turn of the century, the Atchison, Topeka, and Santa Fe Railway set out to build a rustic resort that would fulfill passengers' dreams of the romantic western frontier; they opened El Tovar Hotel in 1905. From the mainline junction at Williams, Arizona, visitors traveled an additional 60 miles on the spur running north. The canyon was masked from view by the uphill tilt of the Kaibab Plateau, but El Tovar's long profile, capped by a Victorian shingled turret, lent a sense of heightened anticipation and drama. In such a remote, isolated setting, this man-made structure presented a magnificent sight, with its mixed stone-and-shingle styles and Victorian decoration.

A Victorian rooftop wooden turret, wrapped in shingles, easily identifies El Tovar's distinctive silhouette from a distance.

Ten years earlier the trip to the Grand Canyon was a grueling affair, an eleven-hour stagecoach ride to a small hotel. The Santa Fe Railway had bought the hotel to accommodate railroad passengers, but plans to enlarge it were frustrated by an early local settler who built a competing hotel nearby. To overcome that vexation, the railroad moved its terminal several hundred feet to the east and began plans for a luxury hotel that would command unparalleled views of the canyon. A branch line off the main railroad was completed in September 1901, and tourists soon began to arrive at the South Rim.

The concept of building grand hotels at great scenic attractions had gained acceptance with the 1903 opening of Old Faithful Inn at Yellowstone. Previously, wood-framed buildings that served as luxury hotels in resort areas were typically sprawling affairs with Victorian overlays. But the railroaders sought a different architectural concept, one that contributed to the way people perceived and experienced the natural scenic wonders that would later be set aside as national parks.

Charles Whittlesey's architectural reputation was already well established when the Santa Fe Railway selected him to design their Grand Canyon hotel. He envisioned a distinctive silhouette for the hotel and planned a building more than three hundred feet long with multiple roofs at different levels to add to its architectural interest, visual appeal, and spatial uniqueness.

A railroad brochure dated 1909 described El Tovar as "combining the proportions of a Swiss chalet and the Norwegian villa." The hotel's style remains steeped in the late-Victorian predilection for the exotic, complete with roof turret, finials, chalet-like balconies and terraces, and varied exterior wall treatments. Whittlesey's use of a base course of boulders, log veneer siding with notched corners, log detailing on the first floor, and rustic interiors created the frontier atmosphere the railroad entrepreneurs were anxious to promote. Logs stained a weathered brown and a roof shingled with wooden shakes merge the building into the gray-green hues of nearby piñon forests and stone outcroppings. The dark exterior color gives architectural weight to the massive volume and silhouette.

A cascade of changing roof forms continues at each end of the three-story wings, where one- and two-story roof terraces provide views north to the canyon and south to the railway station. The upper terraces are visually separated from the log or plank-sheathed walls below by a projecting roof deck; sections of fretwork railing divided by ten-foot-high tapered finial posts and capped by carved trefoils further define the terraces. The one-story terraced wing on the hotel's rim end is extended by two shingle-roofed gazebos, with rustic benches for silently contemplating the view down into the canyon or across to the North Rim.

The grade at the southern end of the hotel drops off down to the basement level of coursed rubble stone, with arched masonry openings repeated at the entrance porch. The dining room, kitchen, and utility rooms of the west wing stretch out into the lush green lawn. Two stone chimneys on the north and south sides of the dining room are flanked by picture windows facing the canyon. A porch also facing the canyon dates from a dining room expansion and the addition of a cocktail lounge in the 1950s.

El Tovar's three-story guest wings with ground floor logs, second floor horizontal planks, and third floor shingled mansard with dormers.

Early promotional material from El Tovar described the experience of arriving at the railway depot and proceeding up a winding path, to be welcomed by a Norwegian gabled entrance skillfully scaled against the massive dark bulk of the hotel. Projecting out over the wide porch steps at the entrance is a sign with the coat of arms of the family of Don Pedro de Tovar. The porch, flanked by stone walls, is filled with rustic rocking chairs facing Hopi House.

The Santa Fe Railway intended El Tovar to be "not a Waldorf Astoria, but more like a big country clubhouse." The visitor was invited to linger in the entrance lobby, named the Rendezvous, a room almost forty feet square and two stories high. "In it the better half of the world may see without being seen—may chat and gossip—may sew and read—may do any of the inconsequential things which serve to pass the time away."

El Tovar's early operator was the Fred Harvey Company. The dark-stained wood walls and timber-and-plank ceiling, emphasizing the hotel's rustic character, were offset by elegant hospitality. As in other locations where the remote setting was tempered by creature comforts, guests were served on luxurious china, with silverware, crystal, and linen in the Norway Dining Room. The railroad shipped in provisions daily, which were prepared under the supervision of "a capable Italian chef once employed in New York and Chicago clubs." Fresh-cut flowers for the dining tables and guest rooms came from a greenhouse built at Grand Canyon Village.

Appreciation for the scenery and hospitality was often expressed in the hotel's guest book. A Los Angeles visitor in 1914 inscribed: "The canyon is beautiful—impossible of comprehension. El Tovar is in a class by itself. Heaven bless Fred Harvey." The extensive luxury sometimes led visitors to confuse El Tovar with the main attraction. John Burroughs, the famous naturalist, claimed that he heard one guest exclaim, "They built the Canyon too near this beautiful hotel."

The hotel began to show its age about the time the railroad era ended in the 1960s. The days of long vacations yielded to the short-term automobile tour. Wear and tear from exposure and generations of visitors began to add up. When El Tovar was acquired by the Amfac Resort Company, the new management decided to restore it to its early elegance and completed renovations and restoration in 1983.

Architects worked from old photographs and blueprints to ensure historical accuracy. The original hand-peeled Oregon log siding had become irreparably weathered, so the entire exterior was replaced with logs from an Idaho mill; energy-efficient windows replaced deteriorated wooden frames; long-absent decorative finials were restored along with scrollwork and railings, and the original dark brown stain was reapplied. Original interiors were largely retained, but requirements to meet safety standards and efforts toward modernization reduced one hundred guest rooms to seventy-seven, each with a private bath.

Rebuilding a seventy-five-year-old National Historic Landmark that sits perched 100 feet from the South Rim of the Grand Canyon required a good deal of courage and $11 million. The new operators of El Tovar Hotel took on the challenge and succeeded admirably.

Hopi House

Architect Mary Jane Colter's Hopi House project for the Fred Harvey Company at the Grand Canyon was a building devoted to sale of Hopi goods and interpreting the Hopi culture. After her success as the interior designer for the Harvey Company's Indian Building at the Alvarado Hotel in Albuquerque in 1902, Colter was called upon to design an Indian building at Grand Canyon. Because the Hopis have inhabited the Grand Canyon area for centuries, she

Mary Jane Colter's ethnographically correct Hopi House for the Fred Harvey Company.

chose a Hopi design. The approved plans were sent to the Santa Fe Railway's Western Division offices in Los Angeles for the production of construction drawings, and Hopi House opened a few days before the hotel, on January 1, 1905.

Located across from El Tovar Hotel, the building was modeled after Hopi pueblos at Oraibi, Arizona. Colter's biographer, Virginia L. Grattan, observed that Hopi House gave Colter, the "opportunity to re-create the distinctive dwelling of an ancient culture and to acquaint the public with the richness and beauty of Native American

Stepped terraces of Hopi House. Its log ladders connect one rooftop with another.

art." Colter's materials and building massing were identical to those of a pueblo structure and successfully met the Harvey Company's commercial interest in mar-

47

keting Native American arts and crafts in an appropriate setting. Much of the building's stone and timber came from the area, and most of the construction was done by Hopi builders.

The interiors are the same primitive Pueblo style as the exteriors. Massive stone walls were covered with adobe plaster, concrete floors were rough-finished to resemble mud floors, and ceilings were made of saplings, grasses, and mud finish resting on peeled logs. Corner fireplaces, small niches in the walls, and small doorway openings framed with peeled saplings were characteristic Pueblo touches. Colter introduced authentic Southwest artifacts, including the Harvey collection of Indian art. A Hopi ceremonial altar, a sand painting, several Indian rooms, and a Spanish-Mexican room were added to sustain the mood Colter envisioned.

Initially, Hopi House was an actual dwelling; some of the Hopis who worked in the building lived on the upper floors. Indian artisans were in the workrooms making jewelry, pottery, blankets, and other items that were offered for sale. In the evening, the Hopis sang traditional songs, and their dancing on the patio at five o'clock became a daily event.

Lookout Studio

Mary Jane Colter's next building for the Fred Harvey Company at Grand Canyon Village was the Lookout Studio. Perched on the edge of the rim west of El Tovar, it was designed for visitors to observe the canyon through the Harvey Company's telescopes, with opportunities to take photographs from a porch. Inside, a small studio was centered on a fireplace alcove and a display area where postcards, paintings, and photographs were sold.

Natural forms in the landscape at the edge of the canyon inspired the design for Lookout Studio.

Unlike the strict ethnographic interpretation at Hopi House, Colter took a more organic approach and adapted the building to the edge of the canyon, letting the surrounding landscape guide the design. Seen from a distance, Lookout Studio blends into the canyon's walls.

The interior of the structure steps down in several levels. Log framing and stonework are exposed; the original ceiling was made of saplings resting on logs. An uncommon touch for Colter's buildings is the light that floods the interior through the windows on three sides.

Bright Angel Lodge

Two 1890s log cabins were incorporated by Colter into the Bright Angel Lodge complex. The Bucky O'Neill cabin, pictured here, was preserved as a guest cabin.

In 1933, the Fred Harvey Company again called upon the architectural services of Mary Jane Colter, this time to design an economy lodge at Grand Canyon Village. The lodge's location was on the historic site of the old Bright Angel Camp, which was a sprawling complex of cabins, tent platforms, and the antiquated Bright Angel Hotel, clustered near the head of Bright Angel Trail. Acquired by the Santa Fe Railway to resolve a struggle with local hotel operators over tourist traffic, the concessioner was now under the close scrutiny of the National Park Service in coming up with a design for the site.

Colter's early design concept was for a series of stone lodges set right on the edge of the rim. The National Park Service rejected the plan, deciding that visitors should have unobstructed access to the canyon rim. Colter then began designs for a pioneer-style log-and-stone complex away from the rim that would incorporate historic buildings already on the site.

Bright Angel Lodge was designed as a small village of cabins centered around a rustic one-story main lodge with shops, lounges, and dining rooms. The large stone-and-log lodge, under a gable roof and broad overhangs, set the tone for the collection of buildings, some connected to the main lodge by pergolas and walkways. Small cabins built of stone, logs, and adobe, with three or four guest rooms, extended west across the site to the mule corral.

Colter's thoroughness in developing a design concept that skillfully incorporated historic structures was unusual for the national parks. Her rigorous attention to the ethnographic precedents set at Hopi House showed that meticulous research and faithful adherence to historic examples could produce architecture compatible not only with the surrounding topography but also with local tradition. One of her greatest challenges was producing pioneer-style architecture that would recall the early days, incorporate several historic buildings, and respect the edge of the canyon rim. Her success illustrated her design versatility. The complex is full of interesting touches that lead the visitor through a rustic complex at a relaxed pace, following the canyon rim to the mule corral which is at the starting point of the famous trail rides.

The rim side of the main lodge is an inviting single-story face of peeled-log walls and paired-log columns supporting a wide overhang. The main lodge lobby is a two-story space with rough wooden walls, a flagstone floor, and a log ceiling with kerosene lamps hanging from the beams. Colter placed an image of a large thunderbird, the Hopi symbol for the "powers of the air," above the fireplace, and it became the trademark for the Fred Harvey Company "Indian Detours," automobile tours from Harvey Hotels.

The results of Colter's meticulous research can be seen in the lodge lounge, with the "geological" fireplace made of canyon stone and where picture windows frame views of the canyon. Relying upon park naturalist Edwin D. McKee's local knowledge, stones in the ten-foot-high fireplace were assembled to begin at the hearth with water-worn stones from the Colorado River and end at the top with Kaibab limestone from the rim. For furnishings, Colter collected authentic pioneer furniture, kerosene lamps, glass shades, and bathtubs. Rare finds included a hobbyhorse belonging to the first American pioneer child born in Arizona and the lobby's seven-foot-tall Jenny Lind wooden cigar-store figure.

Bright Angel Lodge opened on June 22, 1935, after two years of construction. The opening celebration featured an evening of ceremonial tribal dances and cowboy songs. Depression-era travelers welcomed the new, attractive, low-cost lodgings at the Grand Canyon.

Grand Canyon Power House

A powerhouse was needed to supply power and steam to the Fred Harvey and Santa Fe Railway facilities on the South Rim, as well as steam to heat railroad cars in the rail yards. Although removed from the main visitor traffic along the rim, the building is close enough to El Tovar, the depot, and Bright Angel Lodge to merit attention because of its massive volume and unique design. The building is made of reinforced concrete faced with rough-cut Kaibab limestone and was put into operation in 1926. It managed to combine a straightforward industrial function with the qualities of a Swiss chalet in a delightful artifice. *Trompe l'oeil*—purposeful overscaling of the windows, balcony, eaves, and exterior masonry—makes the building appear considerably smaller than it actually is. By taking the familiar details of a Swiss chalet and nearly doubling them, the viewer is deceived into believing that the building is half its actual size. Careful adherence to the principle of overscaling reduces the powerful form and large volume to a deceptively modest element in the landscape.

In contrast to its Swiss Chalet exterior, the building's interior is uncompromisingly industrial in character: exposed concrete floors and walls, with steel framing for columns and roof trusses. The two original Fairbanks-Morse diesel generators are still in place, along with an overhead crane for maintenance. The Power House operations were shut down in 1956, and the building is now used for storage.

National Park Service Buildings

The National Park Service developed a master plan for the Grand Canyon soon after the park's creation in 1919. The Santa Fe Railway and Fred Harvey Company buildings had already established their unique architectural character in memorable and distinctive designs. Only a short distance away from the Park Operations building were the "Norwegian-Swiss villa" El Tovar Hotel and the pueblo-inspired Hopi House. In constructing the **Operations Building** in 1929, the National Park Service turned to a design in the classic Rustic style. Large enough to have its own identity amid the pyrotechnics of the Santa Fe Railway and the Fred Harvey Company buildings, the Operations Building definitely has its own architectural strength.

The original configuration of the Operations Building was an L-shaped, two-story, wood-framed structure. The building was converted in 1931 into the Superintendent's Residence, and a wing was added in 1938. The final composition is a large-scale residence with many of the elements that would later be refined in other park administration structures at the Grand Canyon and elsewhere in western national parks.

Each element contributes to the Rustic expression of the whole design. Materials appear to have been chosen and placed randomly, belying the designer's subtleties. Each has its own place and importance in the composition. Rows of paired casement windows set in the dark-stained lower walls of horizontal planking and upper walls of vertical board-and-batten read as shadowed planes in contrast with the lighter-colored stone masses. Low-pitched roofs add a horizontal emphasis, and wide overhangs cast shadows onto the already-dark walls. Even the choice of dark brown paint for logs and siding and green trim for the doors and windows were decisions made with the utmost care to help the building blend into its natural environment.

The final step in the development of National Park Service administrative buildings at Grand Canyon was the **Post Office**, built in 1934–35. Here, the burden of guiding depression-era projects shows a waning of what had become the highly refined Rustic style. The composition, materials, and building elements of the earlier structures have been diluted. Where stone is used, it is regular in coursing and has finished surfaces; the narrower eaves and projecting log beams carry a roof that more closely resembles a suburban residence than a Swiss chalet. Today it serves as the Magistrate's Office.

The **Tusayan Museum** and Ruin approximately twenty-two miles east of Grand Canyon Village and four miles west of Desert View on Desert View Drive is an example of early National Park Service efforts at interpretation. The partnership of the American Association of Museums and the Laura Spelman Rockefeller Memorial Foundation, which sponsored Yosemite Museum in 1926, supported the design of a museum at the Tusayan Ruins near the South Rim of the Grand Canyon.

Designed in 1927 and opened in 1928, the museum is a representation of traditional Kayenta Anasazi buildings. The rectangular structure (with a 1934 addition) of native stone and projecting timber *vigas* is extended by an observation terrace on the canyon side. An outdoor exhibit of native plantings supplements the museum proper.

Hermits Rest

Seven miles west of Grand Canyon Village, at the end of Hermit Road, is a Colter jewel of ingenious design, uniquely adapted to a special site. Hermits Rest was built for $13,000 in 1914 and is a testimony to the daring of the Fred Harvey Company and the brilliance of their designer. Fred Harvey ran tours by stagecoach to an old trailhead and wanted a small refreshment stand there for the dusty passengers. Several designs were considered, and Colter's primitive building style was chosen.

The structure appears to be a random jumble of stones with a chimney spire growing out of it. The canyon side of the structure has a log-frame roof protruding from the stonework, covering a patio that is separated from the rim by a stone wall.

The interior of Hermits Rest is medieval in character, shaped by the rugged stonework and cave-like space, with dramatic changes in volume and light. On its northern side, the central room is covered by the exposed peeled-log flat roof of the porch. The roof height opens up two stories into the interior to a flat ceiling

of exposed *vigas* (beams) and *latillas* (poles). The windows facing the canyon and in the upper part of the wall provide a subtle source of natural daylight. A huge semi-dome alcove on the southern end of the space shelters an arched stone fireplace. The flagstone floor is stepped up at the alcove for emphasis.

Desert View Watchtower

Mary Jane Colter returned from Fred Harvey work elsewhere in 1930 to design an observation building at the eastern end of the stagecoach tour. Desert View, with its sweeping vista of the canyons, is twenty-five miles east of Grand Canyon Village. To take advantage of the site, Colter conceived a soaring tower seventy feet high in the form of an ancient Puebloan watchtower.

Colter's vision for Hermits Rest was to create a shelter that would resemble a mountain man's stone-and-timber dwelling.

Colter's best design work reflects her dedication to archeology and ethnohistory. For this project she chartered a small plane for gathering information on watchtowers, locating ruins, and then traveling overland to sketch and study the forms, construction, and stonework. After six months of research she built a detailed clay model to study the design and how it would fit the terrain. Finally, she built a

53

seventy-foot-tall wooden tower on the site to test the form and the views she sought from the promontory overlooking the canyon.

The Watchtower's plan provides for two concentric circles connected by gently arched forms. The larger circle and arched portions form the ground-floor lounge; the smaller circle is the thirty-foot-diameter base of the tower. Inside the stonework of the tower is a steel framework built by the Santa Fe Railway. This was no random pile of rocks mimicking a ruin; Colter meticulously selected each exterior stone to provide a rich surface texture.

The ground floor of the Watchtower is a large circular room modeled after an Indian kiva. Colter specified large observation windows, a flagstone floor, stone walls, a fireplace, and unusual furniture made from tree trunks, rawhide, and burls to create a rustic atmosphere.

From the kiva, one ascends to the first floor of the tower interior, the Hopi Room. Here, Colter's intention to link the history of the Hopi Indians with the Grand Canyon was achieved through sand paintings as well as murals

The Indian Watchtower at the eastern end of East Rim Drive. Colter's design concept for the Watchtower required painstakingly careful selection of stone for the walls.

by two Hopi artists, Fred Kabotie and Fred Greer. The murals depict Hopi mythology and religious ceremonies.

Above, the tower's open shaft—surrounded by circular balconies around the wall edges—is connected by small staircases leading to the rooftop observation deck. Benches were placed along the walls for visitors to observe the graceful curves of

Oddly shaped stones protrude from the walls to add texture and vigor to the structure.

the balconies and the play of light on walls of soft rust and mauve. The space is filled with tiers of balconies, prehistoric images, and the mystical quality of the Native American Southwest.

Colter designed a "ruin" to the west of the Watchtower to simulate the typical condition of prehistoric towers found in the region. This was the sort of ruin she had studied when designing the tower, and it lends an air of antiquity. The opening of the complex was celebrated with a dramatic Hopi dedication ceremony on May 13, 1933.

NORTH RIM

Maj. John Wesley Powell's journey down the Colorado and his explorations of the surrounding area resulted in widespread knowledge about the extraordinary scenery to be found in the territory. Adventurous travelers were soon finding their way to the South Rim of the Grand Canyon. Because of its inaccessibility, the North Rim was an exotic destination. Powell wanted to secure assistance for his continued scientific expeditions in the Southwest and urged Thomas Moran to paint a view of the Grand Canyon from the North Rim that would show the public its majestic beauty. Moran's spectacular painting, *The Chasm of the Colorado*, hung in the U.S. Capitol until the 1930s; it is now in the National Museum of American Art.

Industrious Mormon settlers worked to attract tourists to "their" north side of the canyon. Jacob Lake is at the junction of the road west from St. George, Utah, and east from the Marble Canyon crossing of the Colorado River. Wagon trips were offered to intrepid adventurers from Jacob Lake southward across the Kaibab Plateau through forty-five miles of the Kaibab National Forest. Transporting tourists across the canyon from the South Rim to the North Rim did not seem to be a reasonable prospect, and in 1907 a cable car was installed at the bottom of the canyon for a river crossing to reach Bright Angel Point. Travelers who braved the eighty-five-mile stagecoach trip over dusty roads from Kanab, in southern Utah, were accommodated at the Wylie Way Camp, built in 1916. Several years later, National Park Service director Stephen Mather encouraged the development of improved roads in southern Utah. After the first automobile caravan ventured over the Kaibab Plateau in 1909, tourism on the North Rim began to increase.

Grand Canyon Lodge

In 1926, Gilbert Stanley Underwood was at the height of his architectural powers, working on the Ahwahnee Hotel at Yosemite. The Loop Tour projects at Grand Canyon represented a design challenge, as the Union Pacific Railroad sought distinctive Rustic architecture with common elements among the lodges

Above: The original Grand Canyon Lodge on the canyon's north rim. Right: The terrace, fireplace, and staircase of the 1930 building.

on its tour. The railroad wanted to avoid exact repetition and understood the importance of establishing a unique image for each site. The National Park Service was a willing partner.

Underwood, the undisputed master of the grand statement, created a true masterpiece at the edge of the canyon rim. Following the format of the lodges in Zion and Bryce National Parks, Grand Canyon Lodge was not planned to be as large as the Ahwahnee Hotel. Its aim was to provide impressive public spaces—guest rooms were never intended to be part of the lodge. Overnight visitors were to stay in nearby cabins.

The concept was executed by Underwood with boldness and simplicity. A comparison of the presentation renderings for the Ahwahnee Hotel and Grand Canyon

Lodge shows that both are exuberant massings of natural materials set against dramatic landscapes. Overscaled vertical buttresses of local stone ascending to a central tower embrace oversized logs (faux at Yosemite), used as columns in strong rhythms or as infill wall panels. The walls are scaled from ground to upper floors by decreasing the width of bays and sizes of window openings. The wall surfaces are selectively interrupted by projecting balconies and log beam ends.

At Yosemite, the Ahwahnee emphasizes the verticality of the surrounding valley walls; at the Grand Canyon, the Grand Canyon Lodge underscores the sweeping horizontal line of the plateau and layered canyon walls. The lodge's proportions simulate the shapes and sizes of the canyon's outcroppings and mesas; it is uniquely Southwest in concept and execution. The dominating visual line is the horizontal, interrupted by massive vertical "fingers of stone."

Underwood began to design the lodge in 1927, and construction was underway late that year, with the first guests welcomed in June 1928. The quick construction was due to the excellent organization of the Utah Parks Company, even though this was the most challenging construction site on the Loop Tour. Until roads were built over the two-hundred-mile stretch of land between the lodge and the Union Pacific Railroad, materials had to be hauled up four thousand feet from the canyon by aerial tramway. Water also had to be pumped up from the canyon floor.

A fire tragically destroyed most of the original lodge and several adjacent deluxe cabins in 1932. The Utah Parks Company had made a costly decision when they denied Underwood's request

The simpler forms of the reconstruction after the 1932 fire.

to use concrete and steel. Choosing to use timber from company-owned forests proved fateful, for only the stone columns and walls remained after the devastating blaze. Although the lodge was rebuilt during 1936–37 under the guidance of Union Pacific engineers, it was not as architecturally spectacular as the original. The second story and dramatic observation tower were not replaced, and several flat roofs were modified to pitched surfaces.

Despite Underwood's lack of involvement, the reconstruction nonetheless bears his mark. His original plan featured a forecourt with colonnaded porticos—a classical Palladian villa executed with Pueblo/Mission elements. The centered

57

entrance was defined by large double gables projecting as dormers from the main roof. A southwestern version of a wide outdoor corridor wrapped around the courtyard, and the two wings housed a "western saloon" and service areas. The shingled roof was supported by heavy stone columns, expanded at their bases to form low benches. Public spaces were delineated along the edge of the cliffs, and a spacious lobby offered views of the canyon through large windows. Straight ahead from the entrance was the spacious lounge, to the left a recreation room, and to the right a dining room with peeled-log trusses.

Underwood skillfully varied the treatment from the entrance side of the building to the canyon exposure. The more conservative entrance side was classically proportioned, with a regulated line of identical roof pitches and continuous eaves lines to contrast with the dramatic organic stonework of the building's

canyon elevations. Today, in the rebuilt lodge, all walls facing the canyon are still filled with large expanses of windows, and reflected interior light radiates from the surfaces of the buff limestone walls. Floor elevations progressively descend to the outdoor terraces that naturally step down to the canyon rim. The recreation room is a few steps above the lobby; the dining room and lounge are a few steps below the lobby. On a terrace outside the lounge, a mammoth fireplace and chimney of rugged stonework rise three stories high.

The Lodge dining room's exposed wood trusses incorporate Native American motifs.

Interior volumes are light and airy, reducing the transition between inside and outside. Exposed peeled-log roof trusses, a device often used by Underwood, span the public spaces. Large wrought-iron chandeliers and sconces, parchment fixtures, and painted and carved Native American symbols are found throughout the building. At night, the light from the fixtures provides a warm glow against the limestone piers and dark-stained logs.

Underwood assembled the deluxe cabins—eighteen duplexes and five quadruplexes—using similar architectural elements, the plans varying in porches, entrances, and interior arrangements.

One of the most exceptional places to stay overnight in any national park in the country is in one of the deluxe cabins (#302 or #306) on the east side of Grand Canyon Lodge. Perched at the tip of Bright Angel Point, the cabin entrances are about ten feet above a walk along the edge of the canyon rim. Wide rustic porches provide private viewing platforms virtually suspended over the canyon's rim, where you can enjoy an unobstructed panorama of the canyon.

Exterior wrought-iron light fixture.

The architectural treasures in Grand Canyon National Park are in the contrasting ecological zones of the North and South Rims, focused around the spectacular scenery of the canyon. There is great reward in pausing to visit these historic buildings, which are steeped in the history of the earliest Native American inhabitants, Powell's explorations, the railroaders' developments, and the National Park Service's struggle to manage legions of summer visitors. The National Park Service and concessioners have made commitments to conserve and protect the fragile natural and man-made environment, and they have taken valuable strides in the restoration of important structures that suffer from heavy visitor usage.

Underwood's deluxe cabins were thoroughly rustic in style, evoking Adirondack Mountain traditions.

HUBBELL TRADING POST

ARIZONA

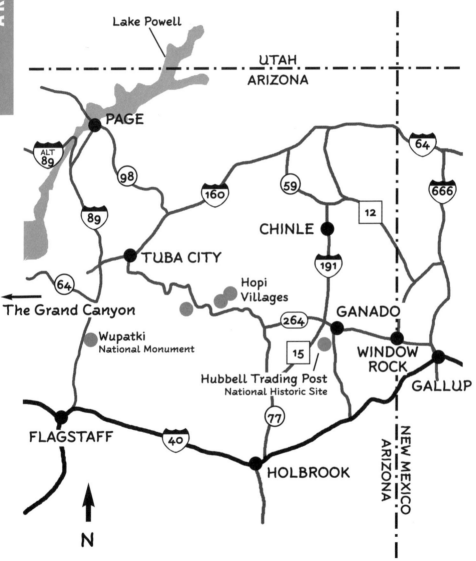

Lake Powell

UTAH
ARIZONA

PAGE

ALT 89

98

89

160

59

12

64

666

CHINLE

TUBA CITY

191

Hopi Villages

The Grand Canyon

64

264

GANADO

Wupatki
National Monument

15

WINDOW ROCK

Hubbell Trading Post
National Historic Site

GALLUP

FLAGSTAFF

40

77

HOLBROOK

NEW MEXICO
ARIZONA

N

5

Hubbell Trading Post
National Historic Site

**Located in northeastern Arizona on the Navajo Indian Reservation
near Ganado, Apache County, Arizona.
www.nps.gov/hutr**

Take exit I-40 at Chambers, go north 26 miles on Highway 191 to Ganado, then one mile west on Highway 264 to the site.

"The first duty of an Indian trader, in my belief, is to look after the material welfare of his neighbors."

John Lorenzo Hubbell, 1907

Hubbell Trading Post at Ganado, proclaimed a National Historic Site in 1965, is a reminder of the days when the reservation trading post was a center for business as well as Navajo social life. Located on the Navajo reservation in northeastern Arizona, the solid stone buildings have changed little since the post's beginnings more than a century ago.

The exile of the Navajos from their homeland in 1864 ended with their return on the Long Walk from Fort Sumner, New Mexico, in 1868. As a defeated people, they became dependent upon traders for supplies in exchange for their wool, sheep, rugs, and jewelry. One of the greatest successes and influences in the Indian trade was John Lorenzo Hubbell.

John
◆———Lorenzo———◆
Hubbell

John Lorenzo Hubbell in 1908

Considered the "dean" of Navajo traders, Hubbell was born in Pajaritos, New Mexico, in 1853. At age sixteen he began his apprenticeship in the trading posts of northern Arizona and southeastern Utah, learning the languages and customs of the local tribes. A settlement at Ganado, founded by an influential chief named Ganado Mucho (meaning "Many Cattle"), attracted Hubbell, and he built a stone-and-log post near Ganado Lake around 1875. Three years later he bought from William Leonard a group of buildings west of Ganado and moved there, where he traded for the rest of his life.

Hubbell claimed 160 acres of land around the post under the homestead laws. At the time, the property was outside the reservation boundaries. In 1880, an executive order enlarged the reservation, and Hubbell found himself surrounded by reservation lands. He made several trips to Washington in efforts to clear his title. Finally, in 1900, Congress passed a special bill legalizing his claim.

Hubbell's success in maintaining the friendship of the Navajos enabled him to expand his operations to include twenty-four trading posts; stage and freight lines; a wholesale business in Winslow, Arizona; and other ranch properties and businesses. He died in 1930, and his son Roman carried on the business until 1957; Roman's wife, Dorothy, ran the store until 1967, when the National Park Service purchased the operation.

Hubbell operated his trading post for more than fifty years, during which time he remained merchant, guide, and friend to the Navajo. The trading post was a place where the Navajos came for news, to meet relatives and friends, and to exchange their goods and crafts for food, tobacco, tools, and cloth. Competition among traders was keen; success or failure could hinge on Navajo tolerance of a stranger in their midst. The trader's currency was not merely the supplies he brought to the Navajos but also how good his word was. The trader

The restored barn, originally built in 1887. Early buildings were constructed of dry masonry, with mud grouting added later.

had to learn the Navajo language and customs, respect their way of life, act as an intermediary between them and the white community, and support them in obtaining government programs.

In the 1870s, Hubbell's reputation was founded on his honesty, trustworthiness, and initiative. He brought Mexican silversmiths to Ganado to teach the Navajos the craft of making silver jewelry. By the mid-1880s, he was encouraging the Navajos to discard careless weaving practices and improve the quality of their work. Under his guidance, they used better wool and developed original designs. The Navajos recognized the benefits of meeting Hubbell's exacting standards, and he gradually gathered the best of the reservation weavers as his suppliers.

The special place that Hubbell Trading Post holds in the history of the Southwest is defined by historian Robert M. Utley in the National Survey of Historic Sites and Buildings Report on Hubbell Trading Post as "the most important single trading post in the history of Navajo trading." Hubbell was one of the first traders on the Navajo reservation, and he influenced the character of trade and traders for more than half a century. He participated in the evolution of a native economy adapted to the conditions of the reservation and the transition in Native American culture that occurred between 1870 and 1920. The origin and development of Navajo craftwork as a profitable industry owe more to his leadership, vision, and guidance than any other factor.

THE TRADING POST: A CULTURAL BRIDGE

The Trading Post's stone-and-adobe buildings began with the main post building sometime in the early 1880s and have remained substantially the same since 1900. The post looks much as it did in Hubbell's time. Minor modifications to the buildings occurred over the years, as doors were added, roofs replaced, parapets raised, and early chimneys replaced by stovepipes.

Trading Post

The long, stone Trading Post building housed the sales room and storerooms for trading. Built in four phases (the office and rug room first, the adjoining storeroom second, the wareroom next, and finally the wareroom extension), the structure is a fine representation of the typical trading post. Walls are made of local sandstone and the roof is framed with ponderosa pine *vigas* and aspen *latillas*. Today, a store with massive counters and grocery-lined shelves still serves the Navajos. The rug room displays blankets, jewelry, antique firearms, pottery, and small paintings of Navajo rugs that line the walls, their origin and use a subject of speculation.

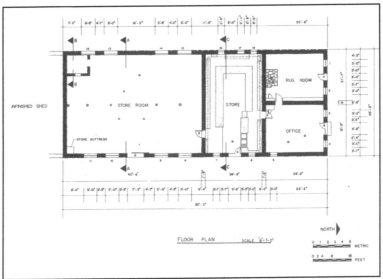

Trading Post floor plan. The approximately 115 feet by 45 feet masonry building was built in four stages from right to left: office and rug room, store, warehouse, and warehouse extension.

The rug room in the Trading Post displays blankets and rugs, jewelry, antique firearms, and a collection of southwestern Indian baskets that hang from the ceiling beams.

Hubbell Hacienda

The hacienda used as the Hubbell family home was completed around 1900. Until then, the family only summered at the post. At the entrance path to the residence, sandstone pillars support a gate decorated with the wrought-iron initials JLH. The rambling, adobe brick building was expanded over the years and grew into a complex of spaces filled with Hubbell's personal collection of Indian art and artifacts. The long living room and bedroom walls are enriched with artwork, photographs, and a profusion of Indian artifacts.

Hogan, Barn, Outbuildings

To the right of the Hubbell home is a stone hogan built as a guest house in the 1930s. A restored barn, begun in 1887 and completed around 1900, and the other residences and utility buildings built of sandstone walls complete the complex. The adobe bake oven produced nearly four hundred loaves of bread a week and stocked the grocery.

Today the National Park Service operates the Trading Post much as it was in the past. The grocery and hardware sales area serve the great-grandchildren of Hubbell's customers and employees across the massive counters where JLH himself once did business. Hubbell Trading Post conveys the remarkable nature of the enterprise that bridged two cultures, the type of man who conducted it, the Native Americans who traded there, and the life they led together.

MONTEZUMA CASTLE

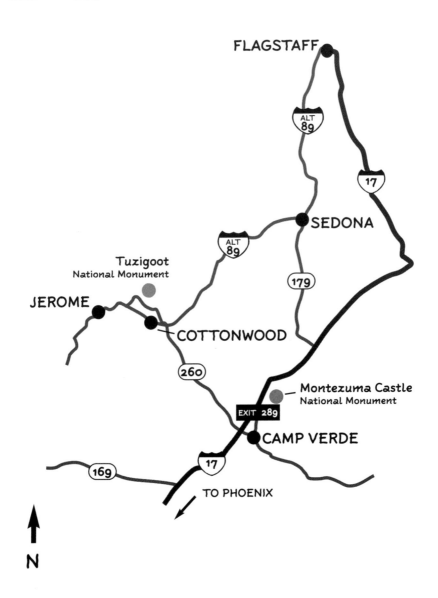

6

Montezuma Castle
National Monument

Near Camp Verde, Yavapai County, Arizona
www.nps.gov/moca

The monument is between Phoenix and Flagstaff, off I-17. Take exit 289 and follow signs 2 miles north to the visitor center.

> "It's not a castle and Montezuma was never here."
>
> National Park Service guide

Montezuma Castle is one of the best-preserved cliff dwellings in North America. Set into a limestone recess more than fifty feet above the floodplain of Beaver Creek in the Verde Valley, the five-story, twenty-room cliff dwelling served as a home for the Sinagua Indians in the twelfth century. With heightened concern over vandalism of fragile southwestern prehistoric sites, the government proclaimed Montezuma Castle a national monument, and it became a major factor in the nation's historic preservation movement. Montezuma Castle National Monument was established in December 1906 and described in the establishment proclamation as "of the greatest ethnological and scientific interest." On April 4, 1947, Montezuma Well, six miles north of Montezuma Castle, was acquired by the federal government through purchase from private owners, and the site expanded to its current 840 acres.

Early settlers to the area marveled at the imposing structure, mistakenly assuming that it was associated with the Aztec leader Montezuma, but in fact the castle was abandoned almost a century before Montezuma was born. The true builders were farmers of the Sinagua culture, migrating from Arizona's northern high country around 1125 and occupying land vacated by some of the Hohokam. Traditionally, the Sinagua were pithouse dwellers and dry farmers. Settlement

patterns in the fertile Verde Valley illustrates the adoption of neighboring cultures by tribes in the region: the Sinagua adopted the
Hohokam's irrigation system, and they began to build aboveground
masonry dwellings in the Anasazi style.

Not an isolated fortress, Montezuma Castle was only one of
dozens of pueblos in a flourishing community along the banks of
Beaver Creek. Protected from the cliff's overhang, the castle survived through six centuries of wind and rain. Other nearby
dwellings did not fare as well. A few hundred yards west of the castle
along the base of the cliff are the badly deteriorated ruins of "Castle
A," once an imposing six-story, forty-five-room dwelling.

There are no absolute dates for the occupancy of Montezuma
Castle. In about 1150, the Sinagua began building their large
pueblos, often on hilltops or in cliffs. Around 1300, the growing
population in Verde Valley was concentrated in about fifty pueblos,
including those at Montezuma Castle and Montezuma Wells.
Probably no more than three hundred people lived in the neigh-
borhood of the Castle at any one time—somewhat more than the
maximum population at Montezuma Well. The Sinagua abandoned
the entire valley in the early 1400s. Scholars have long speculated
over the fate of the Sinagua: Disease? A growing population stress-
ing the land's carrying capacity? Conflict with the Yavapai, who
were living here when the Spanish entered the valley in 1563?
Whatever the reason or reasons, the survivors were probably
absorbed into pueblos to the north.

While the Verde Valley was Spanish and Mexican territory, no
settlements were established in the immediate vicinity of the monument. As a result of the war with Mexico (1846–48), the United
States acquired the Verde Valley. By 1865, enough settlers had come into the valley to warrant the establishment of Fort Verde near the location of present-day
Camp Verde. The earliest date of a pioneer visitor's scratched inscription in
Montezuma Castle is 1880. Army personnel visited the ruin in the 1860s and in
1886 U.S. army surgeon Dr. Edgar A. Mearns dug through debris and bat guano
that accumulated over the centuries.

You can grasp the overall dramatic massing and adaptation to the cliff face
from a viewpoint on the paved trail a quarter mile from the visitor center.
Anchored solidly into a deep alcove in the cliff's curved face, the mud plastered
limestone blocks assembled into terraced rooms truly form a castle-like appearance. Looking upward fifty feet to the castle's lowest level from the trail at the
base of the cliff wall, you can marvel at the esthetic of the Sinaguan—cliff

Montezuma Castle.

dwelling. Like many of the cliff dwellings in the Southwest, the location was chosen for practical reasons. The valley's level land could be reserved for farming, and the pueblo built above the flood plain to avoid disaster. The shady, insulated alcove—cool in the summer—reduced the amount of construction by use of the natural surface as a rear wall. It remained warm during the winter months when the low winter sun heated the walls. All told, it was an ingenious "green" architecture.

Two paths—one leading from the valley floor, requiring ladders, and one from along the face of the cliff—joined at the top of the first ledge to enter the cliff dwelling. Ladders were necessary to enter the building. Montezuma Castle is described as a five-story structure, although there is no place where five stories have been built directly above each other. It is actually a four-story building of seventeen rooms, plus a basement of two storerooms. The building was fitted into the ledges of the natural cave in such a way that it appears terraced. There are two rooms in the first story, four in the second, eight in the third, three in the fourth, and two in the fifth.

The building process started on the ground, and materials were hauled up to the cliff alcove. The walls of Montezuma Castle, two feet thick at the bottom and a foot thick at the top, are chunks of limestone, usually no larger than two bricks, laid in mud mortar of clay and sand mixed with river water. They were carried to the site in baskets up pole ladders. Constructed on the very edge of the ledges with enough earth fill behind to provide level floor space, the walls were covered with mud plaster, both inside and out. Most of this has weathered away on the outside, but the plaster is well preserved inside. In some places, finger marks of the original builders may still be seen. The graceful curve of the walls conforms to the alcove's shape and adds stability to the structure.

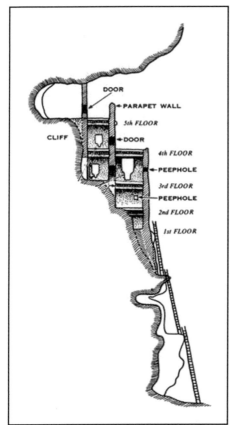

Cross section of the five-story castle.

Building without any metal tools, the builders hewed roof beams from sycamore trees along the river and hauled them up the cliff with ropes twisted from yucca fiber. Some of the roof timbers—one foot in diameter and up to ten feet in length—still bear chopping marks from stone axes with short wooden handles Resting on the main roof timbers and laid at right angles was a covering of poles and bundles of coarse grass or willows, topped by a layer of mud three or four inches thick.

Inside the pueblo, walls made of rubble, covered with mud plaster divide long narrow rooms. Building progressed gradually, with two or three rooms added at a time until twenty rooms on five levels fit into the alcove. A waist-high parapet wall at the top of the castle encloses a patio. Rooms average about 100 square feet. The smallest room is in the second story with 37-1/2 square feet of floor space, and the largest is in the fifth story with 240 square feet. The irregular face of the cliff provides sleeping platforms and niches for storage. A pictograph is incised in the mud plaster on the wall of one room. This roughly rectangular figure measures about six by eight inches, and is laid off into four sections by lines that intersect at the center. In the upper left and lower right quarters are vertical wavy lines that suggest water.

The Castle's exterior is punctuated by a few rectangular openings, possibly to benefit from the insulation of the thick walls, which help the rooms retain the lower temperatures of the natural rock walls in the summer and the heat from fires in the winter. Doorways, sometimes T-shaped, are lower than the then-average male's height of five feet four inches. These wall openings, possibly evolved from the Anasazi culture, keep the heat in and the cold out of interior rooms.

Because of the structure's fragility, the Castle is no longer open to visitors but is visible from the trail at its base. The Montezuma Castle Visitor Center exhibits pottery, textiles, and other artifacts from the site. There is a level paved trail one third of a mile in length and wayside exhibits along a self-guided trail among sheltering sycamore trees. Under a typical brilliant blue sky, the monument conveys the quiet atmosphere of Sinaguan times in this warm fertile oasis found in a spectacular landscape of forested mountain ranges and high mesas.

PETRIFIED FOREST

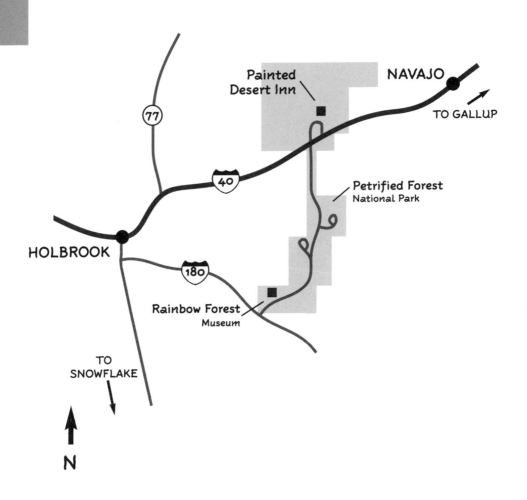

Painted Desert Inn

NAVAJO

TO GALLUP

77

40

Petrified Forest
National Park

HOLBROOK

180

Rainbow Forest
Museum

TO
SNOWFLAKE

N

7

Petrified Forest
National Park

Near Holbrook, Apache County, Arizona
www.nps.gov/pefo

The National Park may be entered from the north at exit 311 off I-40, 25 miles east of Holbrook. The south entrance is 19 miles east from Holbrook on Highway 180.

> "Step out of the car and walk away from the road into the burnished palette of the Painted Desert, into the lunar hills of the Blue Mesa, or among the tangle of fallen logs that marks the petrified forests."
>
> *The Sierra Club Guides to the*
> *National Parks of the Desert Southwest*

Petrified Forest National Park is a marvel of natural wonders forming one of the most unusual landscapes in the United States. The park, designated a national monument in 1906 and redesignated a national park in 1962, is located in the central Arizona desert highlands. It lacks the dramatic features of the crown jewel parks, and Petrified Forest could easily be missed by the traveler hurtling through the desert on Interstate 40. The park is a tourist's treasure, though, for those who find it. An entrance from the interstate leads to the nearby visitor center. From there a twenty-seven-mile-long road loops southward through the unique terrain of petrified logs, prehistoric ruins, badlands eroded by water and wind, and the Rainbow Forest, taking visitors to the Rainbow Forest Museum at the southern end of the park.

Beyond the visitor center, a road curves along a wide mesa and rises over the

The Stone Tree House, built in 1924 by Herbert D. Lore, was converted into the Painted Desert Inn. The site commands sweeping views of the Painted Desert.

edge of the Painted Desert. At Kachina Point, the National Park Service built the superb Painted Desert Inn. A mixture of Spanish and Pueblo styles, this National Historic Landmark Rustic lodge is uniquely representative of southwestern architecture and bureaucratic ingenuity.

Painted Desert Inn

Painted Desert Inn is a gentle orchestration of building masses set on a flat landscape. From a distance, its earth-colored walls and stepped parapets seem part of the surrounding topography. The inn's stucco surfaces take on different color hues, in perfect harmony with the colors of the Painted Desert. In the early morning hours and at twilight, the walls have an orange cast; at midday the sun has bleached them into flat pink.

The inn comes into view gradually from the approach road. Its irregular plan, multilevel construction, and massing of individual rooms anchor the inn comfortably in its site. Partial banking into the mesa edge appears to diminish the two-story structure's volume. Terraces on three sides of the building have low walls that define the outdoor spaces, some overlooking the ever-changing colors of the Painted Desert. Exterior walls are pierced by *viga* ends and *canales* (scuppers), which drain the flat roofs, creating play between light and shadow on the walls.

The fascinating history of the inn begins with a lodge, the Stone Tree House, privately built in 1924. The lands of the Painted Desert north of the Petrified Forest National Monument, including the original lodge, were acquired by the National Park Service in 1936. The monument and the Painted Desert were combined to create Petrified Forest National Park in 1962. The original lodge was constructed of local adobe and petrified logs and contained a trading post, lunch counter, and the owner's living quarters. Unfortunately, the building was constructed on unstable clay soil that damaged the stone walls.

When the National Park Service acquired the lodge, Thomas C. Vint, the

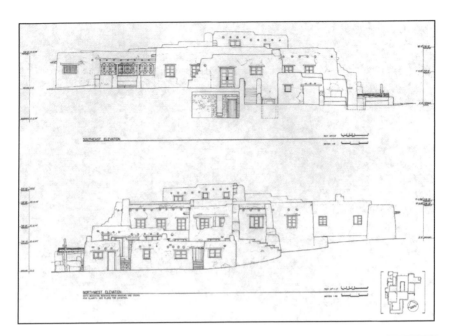

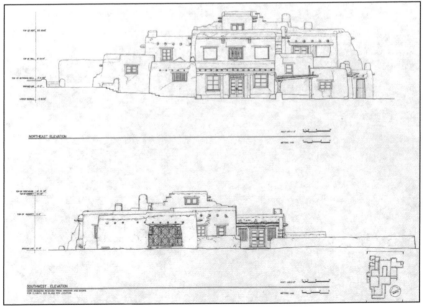

Painted Desert Inn elevations. A variety of volumes, window opening treatment, and the decorative use of vigas, establishes the inn as a significant example of the Pueblo Revival architectural style.

chief architect of the National Park Service Branch of Plans and Design, chose to do a major rebuilding. This strategy was a bureaucratic ploy, for funding was easier to obtain for "rebuilding" than for new construction. When construction funds fell short of contractors' estimates, the National Park Service design staff decided to use the available money to purchase the basic materials and to use labor from the Civilian Conservation Corps (CCC) camp at nearby Rainbow Forest. Construction began in the fall of 1937 and, after considerable travail, was finally completed in July 1940.

Under National Park Service supervising architect Lorimer Skidmore's supervision, CCC crews obtained ponderosa pine and aspen logs for structural members and *vigas* from Sitgreaves National Forest. The crews shaped the logs, carved the corbels, and hewed the *vigas*. In some places, the crews propped up the sagging stone walls, dug underneath them, and replaced the foundations. Flagstone floors were laid in some rooms, and in others poured concrete was stained soft tints and then incised with patterns inspired by those on Indian blankets. The furniture and interior wall colors repeated the same soft colors. Workers plastered around window and door openings in the two-foot-thick masonry walls, narrowing the width at top and bottom by the sweeping motion of their hands to create shapes resembling those in old pueblo buildings.

Skidmore described the building's design as influenced by Pueblo Indian dwellings softened by Spanish Colonial decorative touches. The results of thorough study of these influences are evident in the finished building. *Vigas* and split aspen *latillas* were used in a traditional Puebloan fashion as ceilings, along with adzed *vigas*, carved corbels, and brackets of Spanish Colonial origins. Windows, doors, and frames were sandblasted for an "aged" finish before installation.

When the inn opened, it contained twenty-eight rooms divided between the National Park Service and concessioner's use. The concessioner's space included a lunch room, kitchen, dining room, dining porch, six staff sleeping rooms with corner fireplaces, service areas, and the Trading Post Room. The inn closed in 1963, and the building is now operated as a museum and bookstore by the National Park Service and Petrified Forest Museum Association.

The most magnificent interior space is the Trading Post Room. An enormous skylight with multiple panes of translucent glass painted in designs from prehistoric pottery provides soft illumination over the concessioners' sales items. Six hammered-tin, Mexican-style chandeliers are suspended from ceiling *vigas*, and the posts supporting the corbels and *vigas* are painted in muted Spanish Colonial colors. The masterful combination of the skylight and the highly decorative woodwork on posts, corbels, ceilings, and furnishings makes this building a memorable example of Southwest design.

The inn officially opened in 1940, but its business days were cut short by the onset of World War II, after which it no longer offered guest lodging. After the war, the Atchison, Topeka, and Santa Fe Railway's concessioner, the Fred Harvey Company, took over its operation. The company's architect Mary Jane Colter was brought to the inn to update the building to Fred Harvey standards. She changed the interior color scheme and hired Hopi artist Fred Kabotie to paint a series of murals. Kabotie was a well-known artist, and Colter had previously enlisted his talents for murals at her Grand Canyon buildings. His Painted Desert Inn murals, completed in 1948, incorporated ceremonial and religious symbolism, and some showed scenes from everyday Hopi life. The dining room was dedicated as the Kabotie Room in 1976.

Many people had a hand in creating the Painted Desert Inn—CCC crews, construction supervisor Skidmore, architect Colter, and artist Kabotie—but the credit for its design belongs to National Park Service architect Lyle E. Bennett. His early career with the National Park Service at Mesa Verde was in the ranger ranks, working elbow to elbow with archeologists on excavations, unearthing pieces of the past. With pickax, shovel, trowel, whisk broom, and toothbrush, he scientifically dug up bits of pottery, portions of house walls, and various fragments from a vanished civilization. Part of Lyle Bennett's earliest National Park Service job also included long hours of laboratory work, recording the archeological data, and cleaning and stabilizing artifacts for future study or museum exhibition. This detailed work led to a strong interest in prehistoric pottery, and Bennett studied the subject further. Years later, he drew upon this knowledge when designing the intricate patterns in the skylight of the Trading Post Room.

At the time Bennett was designing the Painted Desert Inn, he had already completed a number of National Park Service buildings in the Southwest. His command of the southwestern idiom was masterful, and he always included design subtleties that made his buildings unique. He used his talent and experience to employ simple building materials to produce an impressive architectural accomplishment in the Painted Desert Inn.

Museum

The Rainbow Forest Museum, built in 1931, has an exhibition room in a sky-lighted raised central block and two symmetrical wings, with beams over the recessed main entrance and windows. The compound entryway's design was based on a series of three rectangular doorways, each a stone's width smaller than the preceding, which drew the eye to the centrally located metal and glass double doors. The outer periphery of the central building had stepped vertical stone extensions that mirrored the doorway. Stone was used for the short wing walls that defined the fan-shaped design of the stone entry steps.

The simple block-like forms of the eighty-foot-long sandstone structure are an interesting merging of styles. In *Park and Recreation Structures*, the building was described thus: "With simple dignity, this building happily succeeds both in capturing the flavor of the architecture of the Old Southwest and in gesturing toward contemporary. This is no mean attainment in itself, and with the added score of an orderly workable plan, it is successful beyond cavil."

A short distance from the Museum visitor center is Giant Logs Trail. A six-mile paved loop leads through the largest concentration of petrified wood in the park. The logs here lie criss-crossed atop each other in log-jam fashion. Most are the petrified remains of extinct conifers. At the north end of the trail are some of the park's longest intact logs, one of which measures 116 feet. The fencing is a reminder that there is a Federal law prohibiting collection of petrified wood.

PIPE SPRING

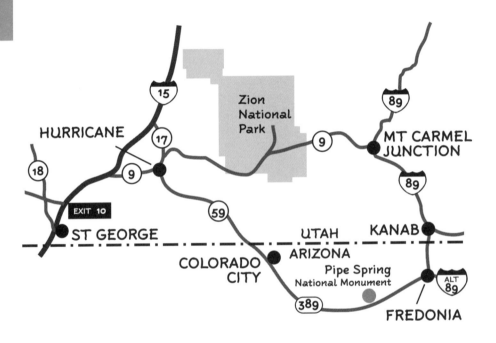

N

8

Pipe Spring
National Monument

Between Fredonia and Colorado City, in Coconino County, Arizona
www.nps.gov/pisp

The monument is in northwest Arizona near the Utah border. From Flagstaff, take Route 89 north towards Page, Arizona. Then take Route 89A 40 miles to Jacob Lake. Continue north on 89A to Fredonia and take Route 389 west to the site. Or from Las Vegas, Nevada, take I-15 past St. George, Utah, to exit 10, on to Highway 9 east to Hurricane, and continue to the monument 60 miles via Utah Highway 59 and Arizona Highway 389.

". . . dedicated as a memorial of Western pioneer life."

President Warren G. Harding's proclamation
declaring establishment of Pipe Spring National
Monument, May 31, 1923

The fort complex at Pipe Spring National Monument was built at a time when the Mormons were settling the Dixie Country of southern Utah and northern Arizona. The red-colored sandstone walls of the fort and outbuildings stand today much as they did when completed in the early 1870s, a reminder of the isolated existence of those pioneers. The visitor center museum has original cooking utensils, plows, and water barrels. Rooms are furnished in period furniture. Costumed guides interpret life at Pipe Springs by demonstrating pioneer activities. The oasis-like nature of the monument can be discovered in a shaded grove, among the geese at the sluice carrying water to the fort's ponds.

Separated from northwestern Arizona by the Colorado River and the Grand Canyon, the grasslands in the midst of this semi-arid country attracted Brigham

The ten by twelve foot portals that served as the fort's main entrance contain huge double doors supported by heavy wrought-iron hardware.

Young as a possible center for cattle ranching. The Mormons pushed south and west from the Great Salt Lake, exploring the area around present-day Cedar City, Utah. In the early 1850s, when iron ore and coal deposits were discovered, settlement began in earnest. Indians defended against the territorial claims, and the fort at Pipe Spring was built to protect the settlers.

The preserved Pipe Spring complex is a place of abundant water in the vast, thirsty land of the Arizona Strip. Free-flowing water from the sandstone layers to the north provided a cool, tree-sheltered oasis that attracted Indians, travelers, and settlers for centuries. Pipe Spring National Monument is one of the few places in the national park system that illustrates the daily life of nineteenth-century ranches.

Jacob Hamblin ◆——— Mormon ———◆ Leatherstocking

Missionaries under the leadership of Jacob Hamblin were assigned the tasks of reconciling differences with the Indians and exploring the Dixie Country. Hamblin's gentle nature and leadership enabled him to succeed in the role of peacemaker with Indian settlements in southwestern Utah. In addition to protecting settlers, the Mormon missionary explorers searched for crossings in the rugged canyons of the region, including the Grand Canyon.

Hamblin was known as the "Mormon Leatherstocking" and is credited with leading the group that came upon Pipe Spring during an expedition in 1858 into the Arizona Strip between the Utah border and the Colorado River in Arizona. Hamblin's marksmanship gave the spring its name. A story relates his attempt to shoot a suspended silk handkerchief. He became frustrated at the elusive target and suggested that a pipe be placed on a rock and he would shoot out the bowl without touching its sides. He did it, and the spring was forever after known as Pipe Spring.

Stockmen soon came to the lush grasslands around the desert oases and established ranches. In 1863, James Whitmore began ranching and built a dugout for temporary shelter. Three years later, Whitmore and his herder Robert McIntyre were killed by Navajos who crossed the Colorado River to drive off the stock. Companies of militia were sent into the area, and Pipe Spring was selected as the base for holding land north of the Colorado River. In April 1870, Brigham Young appointed Anson Perry Winsor to run church affairs in the area, with a promise of a headquarters ranch capable of withstanding Indian attacks.

In September 1870, Hamblin, Young, and Maj. John Wesley Powell met at Pipe Spring. The adventurous major, called "Ka-pud-ats" (One-Arm-Off) by the Navajos, traveled with the Mormon leader from Salt Lake City to meet the Indians and try to negotiate a peace treaty. Maj. Powell was concerned about the safety of his team.

Hamblin had been hired as a guide and interpreter, and at Pipe Spring, plans were made for a fort to protect the valuable water supply, the grazing grounds, and those members called by the church to serve there. A couple of months later, Hamblin and Powell worked out a peace treaty with the Navajos at Fort

Defiance. For the time being, peace reigned on the Arizona Strip, and building began on the fort in late 1870. Winsor was appointed superintendent of the ranch, supervising the construction that began in 1871 and was completed in 1872. The fortress-like structure, more imposing than anything else for miles around, eventually became known as "Winsor Castle."

THE PIPE SPRING BUILDINGS

An inspection of the restored fort, either from a distance or close-up, gives the clear impression of a complex designed and built with protection in mind. No windows faced toward the outside, and the only openings in the massive, two-foot-thick walls of random ashlar red sandstone were pairs of wooden gates in the courtyard walls and gaps between the stones for rifle ports—eight in the north building and fifteen in the south. The tapered gun-port openings provided light and served as observation posts as well. Placing the fort on top of Pipe Spring was a safety feature to protect the water

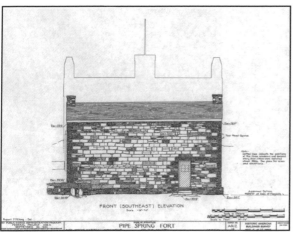

Southeast elevation.

supply. The footings of the northwest wall were built over the mouths of the springs, and the water was channeled in trenches under the floor of the north building into the courtyard and then into a dugout log in the cooler room of the south building and to pools outside the walls.

The fort's two-story buildings, approximately eighteen feet by forty-three feet, form a thirty-foot courtyard enclosed by twenty- to thirty-foot-high walls. Wagons and teams entered the courtyard at either end through massive ten-by-twelve-foot wooden doors. A two-foot-wide cat-walk connects the upper floors on one side of the courtyard. The fort buildings show Greek Revival details that recall the style popular in the 1830s in upstate New York, where the Mormons originally came from. White gable and end-return trim, chimneys at the ends of each building, and a wood-frame clapboard observation cupola on the center of the north building's roof ridge suggest the mixed use of residence and fortress. Multi-light, double-hung sash windows face the courtyard, and raised-panel doors, door-frame panels, and interior paneling add to the Greek Revival ambience. The fort's interesting architectural profile, reflecting the cliffs behind the building, is an accident of the site. Wintertime excavation for the north building proved difficult and was halted when the floor level was still five feet higher than the south building.

The cedar-shingled, shallow-pitched main roof of each building is extended eight feet to cover second-floor verandahs facing the courtyard. The lower floors are of approximately equal size, divided by a stone bearing wall. In the north building, first-floor rooms served as the fort's main kitchen

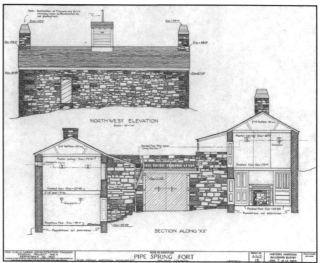

Northwest elevation and cross section. North and south buildings are placed parallel on their long axes. A thirty-foot wide enclosed courtyard was created by connecting the buildings with two-feet-thick stone walls twenty to thirty feet high.

and parlor for family gatherings and social events; the upper floor contained a family bedroom, meeting room, and a guest room with a trapdoor to the rooftop lookout tower. On the south building's ground floor were the spring room and cheese room; upstairs were bedrooms and a meeting room. On a table in the telegraph operator's room is a telegraph key and, above it, a photo of Eliza Louella Stewart. She was eighteen years old when she used the telegraph key to send the first telegraph message from the state of Arizona.

Latter-day Saint church members from the territory helped pay their tithes by working on the fort. Brothers Elisha and Elijah Everett were the head stonemasons; both had previously worked on the Mormon temple in Salt Lake City. At first, construction moved ahead slowly. Skilled blacksmiths, carpenters, and cabinetmakers had to be brought together, housing created, and tools and other supplies shipped in. Readily available sandstone was excavated from nearby cliffs. The masons resorted to the ancient technique of drilling holes along natural fracture lines in the stone, driving in wooden pegs, pouring on water, and letting the swelling pegs split the rock apart. The stones were then drawn to the site, shaped, faced, and hoisted

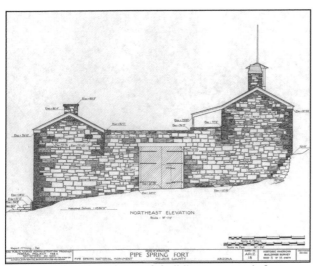

Northeast elevation. The north building was set six feet higher than the south building to fit the sloping hill.

to the top of the walls by block and tackle. Mortar, made from imported limestone, was burned in a kiln on the site. Wagon-loads of rough-cut, unmatched pine planks came from the Skutumpah sawmill.

Before the fort was completed, two smaller buildings were added. The stone-walled one-room structure built by the militia in 1868 was extended by adding another room and connected by a breezeway to house the Winsor family during the fort's construction. The buildings later served as the blacksmith shop and bunkhouse. A second stone structure, built west of the fort, served as a bunkhouse for Maj. Powell's survey crews in 1871. Both were in a state of ruin when acquired by the National Park Service in 1923, but the sandstone masonry walls were rebuilt, and low-pitched log-framed roofs were replaced to match the originals.

National Park Service Acquisition

December 15, 1871, was a day of celebration at the fort: The first telegraph station in Arizona went into service. The line, part of Deseret Telegraph established by Brigham Young and owned by the church, serviced the state of Utah. When Maj. Powell's surveyors arrived, they bore the dismaying news that Pipe Spring was not in Utah, as supposed, but in Arizona.

At about the same time, Bishop Winsor went into the cheese-making business. This was carried out on the south building's lower level; the business produced sixty to eighty pounds of cheese a day. Brigham Young's plans for self-sufficiency were met with butter, cheese, and beef supplied to St. George, or wherever markets were found. When Winsor left the fort in 1875, the dairy business was being replaced by profits from the cattle herds. When danger from Indians no longer existed, part of the courtyard walls and the gates were removed, windows were cut in the massive stone exterior walls, and two water-storage pools were dug to irrigate a large garden and orchards.

The importance of Pipe Spring Fort to the Mormons gradually declined, although it became a popular stopping-off place for gold prospectors, cowboys from the surrounding area, and Mormon couples passing on to St. George for marriage in the Mormon temple there. The site was eventually absorbed by the Canaan Cooperative Stock Company of St. George, Utah, in 1879. It was sold to private owners in 1884, and Winsor Castle became the center of a large cattle-ranching operation in the Arizona Strip. The ranch changed hands several times until it was purchased in 1906 by Jonathan Heaton and Sons from nearby Moccasin. The incorporation in 1907 into the Kaibab Paiute Reservation and complications over water rights made ownership burdensome. A fortuitous meeting with National Park Service director Stephen Mather in 1922 gave Charles Heaton the opportunity to relinquish the property by suggesting Pipe Spring as a national monument commemorating the part the Mormons played in opening the West.

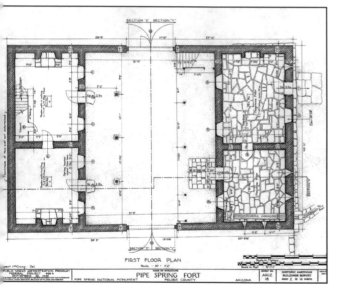

FIRST FLOOR PLAN

PIPE SPRING FORT

The compact enclosure provided protection for the settlers. However, this protection never proved to be necessary.

Sites in southwestern Utah had already caught the interest of assistant National Park Service director Horace Albright. Stephen Mather became interested in Pipe Spring as Zion, Bryce, Cedar Breaks, and other regional parks and national monuments were coming under National Park Service supervision. In a creative deal, Heaton sold the ranch to the threesome of Mather, Heber J. Grant (president of the Mormon Church), and Carl Gray (president of the Union Pacific Railroad). The new owners deeded the land to the government, and in 1923, President Warren G. Harding proclaimed Pipe Spring a National Monument to serve as a "memorial of western pioneer life." Pipe Spring became the first designated historic site in the national park system and assured the preservation of this unique remnant of Mormon history and settlement.

TUMACACORI

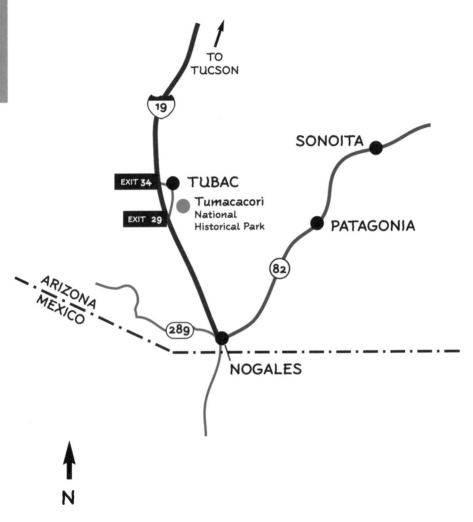

TO
TUCSON

19

SONOITA

EXIT 34   TUBAC

Tumacacori
National
Historical Park

EXIT 29

PATAGONIA

82

ARIZONA
MEXICO

289

NOGALES

N

9

Tumacacori
National Historical Park

Located near Tumacacori, Santa Cruz County, Arizona
www.nps.gov/tuma

Tumacacori in southern Arizona, near the Mexican border, is 18 miles north of Nogales and 45 miles south of Tucson. Take I-19 and exit 34 from the north, and exit 29 from the south, and follow signs to the visitor center.

"We had intended to circle back from Tucubavia to Cocospera, but messengers . . . from San Cayetano del Tumacacori came to meet us. . . . The father Visitor said to me that the crosses they carried were tongues that spoke much and eloquently, and that we could not fail to go where they summoned us."

Father Eusebio Francisco Kino, January 1691

The white plastered sanctuary dome of the Mission of San Jose de Tumacacori provides a shimmering landmark at this national monument in southern Arizona. The mission has been only partially rebuilt since its abandonment in 1844. The juxtaposition of the mission ruins and the finely crafted Spanish Colonial museum and visitor service buildings added by the National Park Service in 1937–39 provides a unique interpretive perspective on the early settlement of the region. Proclaimed a national monument in 1908, the forty-six-acre site was redesignated a National Historical Park in 1990.

The sound of mariachi bands at Sunday masses and demonstrations by Native Americans and Mexicans participating in the park's living history programs capture the Spanish–Native American culture of the old Southwest.

The restored white plaster dome with raised steps for access to the lantern. The lantern is a decorative detail that does not communicate with the interior.

The Mission

The original mission plan followed the traditional Franciscan organization of space for spiritual and temporal affairs. A church, residence for the padres, a dormitory for unmarried women *(convento)*, shops, quarters for a military escort, mortuary and burial ground, and storerooms all enclosed a courtyard *(patio)*. Massive adobe walls were extended to enclose the Indian village of Tumacacori.

Construction consisted mainly of adobe or burned bricks. Oriental influences from Spanish mid-sixteenth-century architecture, filtered through Spanish Colonial experiences in Mexico, can be seen in the sanctuary dome and polychrome decoration on the ornate façade. The powerful entrance façade, meant to project over the proposed vault of the nave, unlike those on mission churches farther away from Mexico, was created by modeled plaster decoration over adobe. A twin tracery of projecting adobe-brick forms a framework around the edge of the façade, focusing attention on the arched entrance defined by heavily plastered columns and radial arch stones to simulate stonework. The entrance is flanked by a pair of columns—with recesses in between for statuary—that support a beam for the choir loft floor on the interior. The column-and-beam motif repeats on a smaller scale above the beam, and supports a pair of engaged columns framing a statuary recess, an architrave, and an oddly proportioned broken pediment.

The ◆— Mission's —◆ History

Tumacacori Mission ruins in 1936, before restoration.

To establish the Catholic Church among the Indians, seventeenth-century Jesuit missionaries traveled the desert and Sonora highlands of present-day Arizona and northern Mexico, building churches and establishing villages. Their goals were to convert the Pima Indians and consolidate the king's hold on New Spain. An energetic priest, Father Eusebio Francisco Kino, celebrated mass in 1691 at a site several miles away from the Mission of San Jose de Tumacacori, south of Tucson and twenty miles north of the Mexican border settlement of Nogales. A village grew up around the site, and after the Pima Rebellion of 1751 and the expulsion of the Jesuits, the village was moved to its present location. The Franciscans assumed the Jesuits' work, and around 1772, missionary work was consolidated in the district of Tumacacori as a result of continued Apache raids in the Santa Cruz Valley.

Construction of San Jose de Tumacacori began around 1800, and the church was in use by 1820. After Mexico won independence from Spain in 1821, most of the frontier missions were abandoned because of the new government's inability to protect them against Indian raids. Lack of government support led to the sale of the Tumacacori mission to a private citizen in 1844. The church was abandoned, and, until its designation as a national monument in 1908, its only protection against weather and vandals was its adobe construction, with walls up to nine feet thick.

The entrance façade shows how Spanish Baroque forms were adopted into the traditions of the Sonoran desert. The bell tower of the elegant composition was never completed.

The church interior is a long rectangular nave with a domed sanctuary sheltering the main altar and statue of Saint Joseph, patron saint of the church in Franciscan times. The style of the Baroque churches was to focus attention on the altar by means of sanctuary decoration and lights streaming through the clerestory windows below the dome. The church provided a dramatic transition from the bright outdoors to a dim mysterious interior. The transition from the City of Man to the City of God was emphasized by the axial composition and careful placement of clerestory windows and lighting. The contrast of the light-bathed sanctuary and the dimly lit nave emphasized the mystery of communion and the Mass.

The flat-roofed nave has an exposed ceiling of ponderosa *vigas* and planks, with a procession of altars, pilasters, and niches along the walls leading to the pulpit. In the nave, traces remain of holy-water fonts at each side of the entrance, oval depressions in the walls for Stations of the Cross, and symbolic paintings and designs. The outline on the sanctuary wall marks the location of the altar screen. Small windows above the side altars softly illuminate the nave with morning and afternoon light. A barrel-vaulted sacristy is to the right of the nave.

The white plaster dome over the altar, stabilized as part of ongoing restoration, contrasts with the unfinished bell tower. Appearing hemispherical in shape as it rises, the dome's base is not a true circle. On the interior, the base of the dome still shows its painted classical detail.

The uncompleted mortuary chapel behind the chapel in the *Campo Sancto*, the holy field, was a rotunda designed to carry a dome. The holes around the exterior of the chapel's adobe-washed walls were used to support scaffolding for catwalks used by the builders. The field served as the mission cemetery, but after the mission was abandoned, cattlemen used the enclosure as a roundup corral. Cows destroyed the original graves, and grave looters did additional damage. After the Apache Wars, settlers gradually came back to Tumacacori, and the sanctified grounds were restored to their original use. The last burial in the *Campo Santo* was in 1916, and a floral wreath is placed on each grave on every All Saints Day.

The sanctuary interior, brightly lit by daylight from high windows under the dome. Remnants of plaster with painted detail cling to the adobe.

The Museum and Visitor Center

The ruins of San Jose de Tumacacori Mission came under federal protection in 1908, but minimal restoration or interpretive efforts ensued. The desire to improve the site in the early 1930s raised questions about how to handle the remains of the adobe mission structures. Rather than launching a restoration and reconstruction program based largely on speculation, as the Public Works Administration had done at the Alamo, officials decided to preserve all the mission structures and focus on interpretation. The design and construction of a combined museum/visitor center to implement this concept began in 1935.

The proposed Tumacacori Museum presented an unusual set of problems to the Plans and Design branch of the National Park Service. Up until that time, the major body of Rustic work had been in areas where stone and logs were the appropriate building materials. Following the ethic of using on-site materials and indigenous construction techniques to create architecture in harmony with its setting, the designers turned to local culture and southwestern building traditions for guidance.

The National Park Service head of Southwestern Monuments, Frank Pinkley, had definite ideas about the design concept and how to proceed with it. He pictured a utilitarian building, low in height to avoid interfering with views of the mission complex, a "pleasing" but not too ornate façade, and construction techniques, materials, and decorations found in other Sonoran missions in the region. Pinkley also proposed a "view room" from which visitors could look out onto the mission complex, and he set the axis of the building at a particular angle so that visitors would see his chosen knockout view.

A team of National Park Service architects, engineers, technicians, and photographers were dispatched to Sonora, Mexico, in October 1935 to record the remaining mission structures in the Kino chain and to study construction techniques and architectural elements under the direction of the principal designer of the museum, Scofield DeLong. The researchers' stay was cut short because of rebel uprisings in the region. The research nonetheless provided invaluable documentation, and DeLong incorporated many of the elements that he had seen in the Sonoran missions into his design for the museum building. Construction began on the museum building in 1937. All work, including the garden, was completed in 1939.

A seven-foot adobe wall extending north and south from the museum's west wall screens all but the upper portions of the mission ruins from the road and parking lot, and channels visitors toward the museum's main entrance. A T-shaped plan of 5,500 square feet houses the museum. Arcades extend from the east wing—one opening into the garden and the other providing views of the church ruins. The patio garden, begun in 1939, contains plantings similar to those grown in the missions of northern Sonora.

In proper National Park Service tradition, architect DeLong chose construction materials and decorative elements found in other Sonoran missions. Walls were built of sun-dried adobe bricks, with cornices of fired bricks. The flat-roofed building is surrounded by a parapet with a stepped coping, and is drained by channels cut into the adobe piers of the portals. The scallop-shell motif over the main entrance, symbolizing Santiago de Compostela, patron saint of Spain, was patterned after the church entrance at Cocospera in northern Sonora, Mexico.

The main entrance door of the museum, carved by Civilian Conservation Corps craftsmen at Bandelier National Monument, incorporates floral designs used at San Ignacio in Sonora, Mexico. The museum lobby has a fireplace in the southeast corner and a floor of large bricks laid in a herringbone pattern. Carved corbels and the beamed ceiling are similar to the nave ceiling of Oquitoa, and the lobby counter follows the design of the confessional at Oquitoa. The room also features handmade Spanish Colonial furniture. Of the several museum rooms, the "view room" is architecturally the most important. An arcade on one side—with piers and arches copied from those at Caborca—frames views of the mission. Groin-vault ceilings were frequently used in Sonoran missions—at San Xavier, Tubutuma, and in the baptistery at San Ignacio. The open-air room contains a scale model of the mission for comparison with the stabilized ruins.

The National Park Service's goal for the design of the museum building was to replicate the mission architectural style from around 1800 for living and working quarters. Rather than follow the archeological and ethnographic designs of Mary Jane Colter, the designers and museum staff created a structure to illustrate mission development and to act as a model of historic construction techniques and materials. The impressive museum building at San Jose de Tumacacori attests to their success and has been designated a National Historic Landmark.

TUZIGOOT

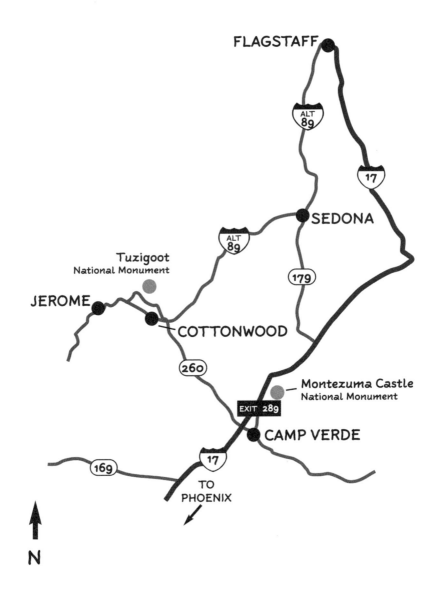

FLAGSTAFF

ALT 89

17

SEDONA

ALT 89

179

Tuzigoot
National Monument

JEROME

COTTONWOOD

260

Montezuma Castle
National Monument

EXIT 289

CAMP VERDE

17

169

TO
PHOENIX

N

10

Tuzigoot
National Monument

Clarkdale, Yavapai County, Arizona
www.nps.gov/tuzi

The monument is 90 miles north of Phoenix and 52 miles south of Flagstaff, accessible from I-17. Take exit 287 north to Cottonwood via Hwy 260, continue on U.S. 89A to Clarkdale, and take the access road to the visitor center. An alternate route is from Flagstaff along scenic U.S. 89A through Sedona and to the park.

> ". . . to take advantage of the most commanding place possible . . . for protection or for sheer beauty of location."
>
> Louis Caywood and Edward Spicer, *Tuzigoot: The Excavation and Repair of a Ruin on the Verde River Near Clarkdale* (1935)

The restored ruins of Tuzigoot (pronounced TOO-zi-goot), perched atop a limestone and sandstone ridge high above Arizona's Verde River, is the remnant of one of the largest pueblos built by the Sinagua between A.D. 1100 and 1450. Taking the name from an Apache word for "crooked water" because of nearby crescent-shaped Peck Lake, the ruins have a commanding view over the landscape.

Gradually deteriorating and under depredations from vandals and looters, the site was excavated as a Federal Emergency Relief project in the 1930s. The unusual nature of the hilltop town's excavated ruins and recovered artifacts drew the National Park Service's interest. The owner of the land, mining company United Verde/Phelps Dodge, transferred the site to the federal government, and in 1939 Tuzigoot and the forty-three surrounding acres were declared a national monument.

The restored ruins of Tuzigoot National Monument. Civil Works Administration crews excavated and restored the ruin in 1933–35.

The pueblo's profile against a brilliant blue sky recalls picturesque hilltop villages in southern Europe: an organic architecture of local building materials in a terraced effect, discernible only by the irregular profile and slight contrast of hue from the ridge. The commanding presence of the pueblo suggests that it was built as a fortification, an explanation for many Italian and Spanish hill towns. Certainly there was a hostile environment to contend with, and few exterior wall openings support the concept of self-defense. However, excavations show no signs of events attributed to conflicts with marauding tribes. The hilltop preserved fertile valley land for farming and provided a center for community life, a tranquil and sociable place evident by the rich treasure of artifacts

recovered from the site.

The Verde Valley's first permanent settlers were Hohokam people (Pima for "those who have gone"), who arrived around A.D. 600 to farm in the warm climate and fertile soils, watering their fields by irrigation. Another people in the area were the Sinagua (Spanish for "without water"), pithouse dwellers and dry farmers dependent on rain for their crops. By A.D. 1125, the Hohokam had left the region to the Sinagua, who adopted the Hohokam irrigation system and began to build above-ground masonry buildings that may have been adopted from the Anasazi to the north.

Building form and materials at Tuzigoot follow basic shelter patterns in Southwest Anasazi pueblos: simple cubes of space sharing multistoried common walls of readily available material, wood poles for floor and roof construction, and mud-plastered interior walls. Tuzigoot represents the vestiges of one of several such pueblo communities in the

Tuzigoot's builders used readily available, light-colored limestone and sandstone rough blocks laid in mortar, and in places used smaller pieces of rock to close joints.

vicinity. At maximum size the pueblo may have had nearly ninety rooms and housed as many as two hundred people. Unplanned as a village, the pueblo grew by attached rooms, sometimes built over collapsed earlier structures.

Knowledge of the site comes primarily from the first full-scale excavation at Tuzigoot by two young University of Arizona graduate students, Louis Caywood and Edward Spicer. Supported by Federal Emergency Relief funding (first as a Civil Works Administration and later as a Works Project Administration [WPA] survey), they began work in 1933 with eight men. By 1935, they had excavated the main block of rooms and numerous small surrounding units. They exposed 86 rooms of an estimated 110, and encountered several hundred burials near the main building. The excavators postulated three distinct periods of growth and expansion.

The pueblo community began as a cluster of a dozen small rooms on the ridge top's north-south line for about fifty persons. These rooms, with the exception of one large room, measured seven feet by ten feet. In the next phase, around the year 1200, eight more rooms were built over the ruins of the small rooms along the west side of the ridge top. In the final expansion of growth, between 1300 and 1400, progressively larger rooms were added down the south and east slopes and below the north end of the ridge. Entrances to the rooms were by roof openings and ladders.

In July 1935, the fieldwork and ruin stabilization had been completed with WPA labor, and a 119-page illustrated report was published by Caywood and Spicer, an extraordinary accomplishment in a short period of time. Caywood continued his thirty-four-year career as a distinguished archeologist with the National Park Service, leaving a legacy of meticulous fieldwork and valuable reports.

When excavation at Tuzigoot stopped, floors and masonry walls were pre-served, and several rooms restored for public display. In 1935, with additional federal funds, a museum was constructed nearby to house and display the collection of artifacts from the ruins. One of the few museums interpreting ancient Sinaguan culture in Arizona, the building re-creates the ruins' appearance. The main building, approximately twenty-five by forty feet, is faced with stone rubble, possibly from the excavation. The original roof structure replicates the ruins' assemblage of timber beams and posts, overlaid with poles and bundles of reeds, grass, and bark. The museum's collection in the original 1930 cases presents the story of the Sinaguan farming village, with artifacts from the ruins and other southwest sites.

The Ruins Trail loops around the pueblo and allows visitors to closely view the structures. Remember that the ruins are fragile like other stabilized south-western sites. Follow the trail and don't sit or climb on walls.

WUPATKI

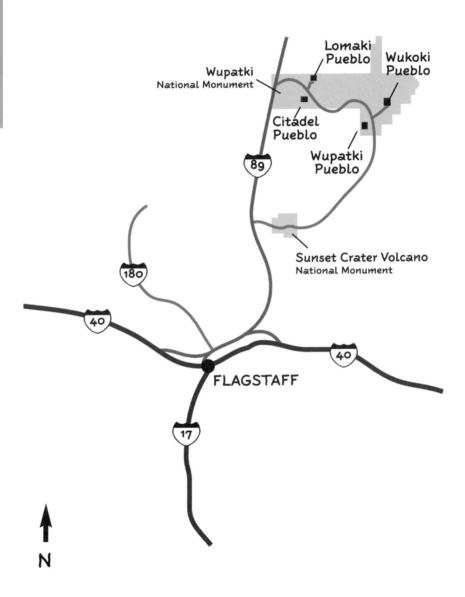

Lomaki
Pueblo

Wukoki
Pueblo

Wupatki
National Monument

Citadel
Pueblo

89

Wupatki
Pueblo

Sunset Crater Volcano
National Monument

180

40

40

FLAGSTAFF

17

N

11

Wupatki
National Monument

North of Flagstaff, Coconino County, Arizona
www.nps.gov/wupa

From Flagstaff, take U.S. 89 north for 12 miles. Turn right at the sign for Sunset Crater Volcano / Wupatki National Monuments. The visitor center is 21 miles from this junction.

> "Leaving the river then, we found . . . all the prominent points occupied by the ruins of stone houses of considerable size. They are evidently the remains of a large town, as they occurred at intervals for an extent of eight or nine miles. . . ."
>
> Captain Lorenzo Sitgreaves Expedition,
> at Camp No. 14. October 8 [1851]

Wupatki National Monument lies atop a windswept mesa northeast of the San Francisco Peaks in northern-central Arizona. Wupatki is the only known location in the Southwest where physical evidence from archeologically separate ancestral Puebloan cultures is found together in more than two thousand Indian ruins built between A.D. 500 and 1400. Located at the crossroads between Sinagua, Cohonina, and Kayenta Anasazi cultural traditions, the monument melds traditions from all these cultures. Preserved at the monument are ruins of red sandstone pueblos built by Ancestral Pueblo people. Wupatki, Wukoki, Lomaki, Nalakihu, and Citadel ruins are easily accessible from the loop road in the 35,442-acre monument, designated in 1924.

Nine hundred years ago, the land was first settled by the Anasazi and Sinaguan people, forming a large agricultural community that spread across this volcanic plateau. They lived in partly underground pithouses and tilled

Wupatki Pueblo ruins.

the soil in those few areas with suffi-cient moisture to support corn and other crops. The eruption of Sunset Crater in A.D. 1064–65 forced many to flee, but it also improved the farming potential: the volcanic ash, blown by winds over a large area, acted as a water-conserving mulch.

After about 1110, people moved back to the area and settled twenty miles north of Sunset Crater in Wupatki Basin. The greatest population growth occurred during the years between 1130 and 1220, estimated to reach approximately two thousand people. Occupation of the most well-known aboveground pueblo ruins dates between 1150 and 1250. A mix of cultural traits can be seen at Wupatki, including Kayenta Anasazi, Sinagua, Cohonina, and Hohokam. Large multistoried pueblos replaced the brush shelters and pithouses of former times. Parrot skeletons, shell jewelry, copper bells, and foreign pottery found at

various sites indicate the prehistoric residents of Wupatki engaged in an extensive trade system with other cultures.

Nineteenth-century travelers such as Captain Lorenzo Sitgreaves and John Wesley Powell marveled at the ruins of pueblo-building tribes on the volcanic landscape of the San Francisco Plateau. "Widely scattered over the region," Powell observed, "thousands of little dwellings are found, usually built of blocks of basalt." Tree-ring data sets 1218 as the time when abandonment of the entire region had likely begun. By 1250, the pueblos stood empty.

Pueblos in the region ranged from one-story, single-family structures to the Wupatki Pueblo. Readily available slabs of sandstone and limestone, chunks of basalt set with a clay-based mortar, and logs from the nearby forests were ideal for the construction of free-standing masonry dwellings. The distinctive red color comes from the dominant local Moenkopi sandstone.

Wupatki Pueblo, the largest dwelling in the monument, was once the home of three hundred people and contained about one hundred rooms. The multi-storied ruins are situated on the edge of a small plateau and have unobstructed views eastward toward the Painted Desert and the Little Colorado River. Walls were two feet thick, and individual rooms six feet high in places. Some walls on the north and west sides extended higher to protect against prevailing winds. Roofs, supported by masonry walls and timber posts, were thick assemblages of large beams, cross-laid with smaller beams, bundles of grass, reeds and bark, and overlaid with a mud topping. There were no exterior doorways at ground level, and rooms were entered through openings in the roof and ladders.

Wupatki Pueblo ruin with ball court to right.

The twelfth-century pueblo stood three stories high in places.

A nearby oval-shaped, smooth-floored amphitheater, where village meetings and ceremonies may have taken place, lies to one side of Wupatki Pueblo. The masonry ball court at the far end of the village, reconstructed by archeologists from wall remnants, may have been used for games or religious functions. It's one of several found in northern Arizona, probably introduced by the Hohokam culture of the southern deserts. A blowhole, one hundred feet east of the ball-court, may have had religious importance. This natural surface opening is a vent of unknown depth linked to underground caves that either blows out or sucks in air, depending on the atmospheric pressure.

The other four main ruins are also accessible by short trails; another impressive site is the Lomaki Pueblo, towards the north end of the park road. It is built right on the edge of a little canyon, which was probably formed by faulting or other volcanic activity, and has a good view of the San Francisco Mountains to the west. Several smaller ruins may be visited along the same trail.

The Wupatki ruins offer a glimpse into the changing attitudes and policies towards restoration and stabilization of Southwest ruins. In the early 1930s, Museum of Arizona archeologists working with Hopi workmen cleared fallen and drifted debris and restored two rooms. Walls and doorways were rebuilt and roofs added, simulating the original twelfth-century

Cleared of debris, some of the more than one hundred Wupatki Pueblo rooms were rebuilt.

masonry and roof construction. The rooms were outfitted for modern living and occupied by park rangers. In the 1950s, the National Park Service established a policy of concentrating on stabilizing ruins and removing earlier reconstruction work. At Wupatki ruins, the restored walls and roofs were removed, and in the 1970s Portland cement mortar was replaced with an amended mud mortar containing Rhoplex.

An attraction among the ruins found on flat-surfaced basaltic rocks is many Anasazi petroglyphs, especially in the vicinity of Crack-in-Rock ruins. The petroglyphs depict humans, a variety of birds and insects, and many graphic designs, including large spirals—Hopi and Zuni symbols thought to represent migrations.

Wupatki Pueblo Trail, located at the visitor center, is a self-guided tour of the largest pueblo in the park. Seven of the best-preserved pueblos have road and trail access; all other sites and the monument's backcountry remain closed to visitors except for seasonal ranger-guided hikes to Crack-in-Rock ruins. The visitor center contains pottery, tools, jewelry, and other artifacts of early cultures. A reconstruction of a Wupatki room shows how the interior of a typical living chamber might have looked. Remember to stay off the walls and don't sit or climb on them.

NEW MEXICO

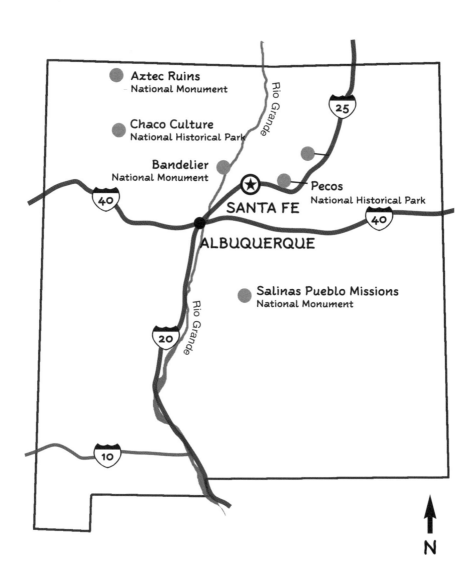

Aztec Ruins
National Monument

Chaco Culture
National Historical Park

Bandelier
National Monument

Rio Grande

25

Pecos
National Historical Park

40

SANTA FE

40

ALBUQUERQUE

Salinas Pueblo Missions
National Monument

Rio Grande

20

10

N

AZTEC RUINS

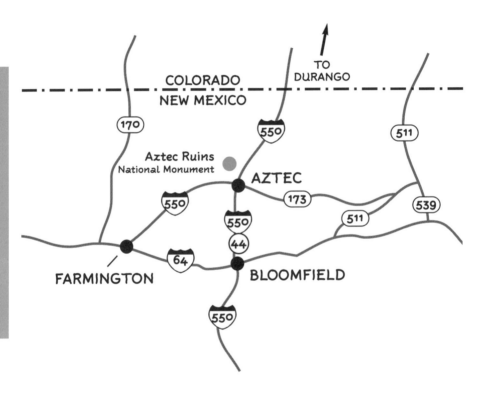

COLORADO
NEW MEXICO

TO DURANGO

170

550

511

Aztec Ruins
National Monument

AZTEC

550

173

511

539

550

44

64

511

FARMINGTON

BLOOMFIELD

550

N

1

Aztec Ruins
National Monument

Aztec, San Juan County, New Mexico
www.nps.gov/azru

Aztec Ruins National Monument is located in the northwest corner of the state, 15 miles east of Farmington on Highway 550, or 8 miles north of Bloomfield on Highway 544. In Aztec, take Ruins Road north off Highways 550 and 544 one-half mile to the ruins.

> "I do not hesitate to say that the excavation of the Aztec ruins would yield a larger and better collection [of artifacts] than has ever been taken from one site in the Southwest."
>
> Earl Halstead Morris to
> John Max Wulfing, February 14, 1916

The Animas River flowing through northwestern New Mexico was a hospitable place for the Ancestral Pueblo people, who settled here eight hundred years ago. Aztec Ruins National Monument illustrates the skills of that people in building community architecture through the large, multistory pueblo on rising ground overlooking the river. The ruins are significant for their blending of the Chacoan and Mesa Verdean cultures, which were here between the twelfth and fourteenth centuries.

Inspired by the popular histories of the 1800s about Cortez's conquest of Mexico, early Anglo settlers named new communities in the vicinity of Indian ruins after native tribes south of the border. So it was with the town of Aztec and, in turn, the ruins became known as the "ruins at Aztec" or, simply, the Aztec ruins. In fact, the rise and fall of the Ancestral Pueblo people preceded the Aztecs by several centuries.

Spanish expeditions passed near the ruins without recording visits and, in 1859, Dr. John S. Newberry visited the undisturbed ruins before pothunters and vandals carried away artifacts and building materials for the next half century. Protection of the site occurred with private ownership in 1889; in 1916, the ruins came under the supervision of the American Museum of Natural History, followed by an intensive six-year period of excavation and stabilization led by archeologist Earl Halstead Morris. Designated Aztec Ruins National Monument in 1923, the site grew to its current 317 acres. Additional recognition came in 1987 when the United Nations included Aztec Ruins with Chaco Culture National Historical Park as a World Heritage Site.

Visitors to the Aztec Ruins National Monument can see a remarkable wealth of ruins concentrated near the visitor center. Besides the principal features of the E-shaped West Ruin and the visitor center, five other major complexes of rooms and structures and at least a half dozen mounds are located within the site. You should get an introduction to the site by viewing the collections in the visitor center before taking a tour of the ruins along the self-guided trail. Remember to duck for the low doorways, and

This band of decorative, greenish stone originally was covered with plaster.

The West Ruin had about 400 rooms and stood three stories high in places. The pueblo includes Chacoan and Mesa Verdean building techniques.

stay on the trail and off the ruin walls. Visits to Chaco Canyon (Chaco Culture National Historical Park, 65 miles to the south) and Mesa Verde National Park (40 miles to the northwest in Colorado) can help you gain an understanding of the influences on the Aztec Ruins site by these two Ancestral Pueblo people cultural centers.

Earl
◆——— Halstead ———◆
Morris

Few southwestern archeological sites are more identified with a single individual than is Aztec Ruins with Earl Halstead Morris. He first came there in 1895 as a child of six and later remembered the exact room he and his father had entered. As a youth, with shovel over shoulder and trowel in hip pocket, he accompanied his pothunting father in the Animas River Valley. Recently graduated from the University of Colorado, he persuaded the American Museum of Natural History to undertake the excavation of the largest of the Aztec Ruins and to put him in charge of a proposed five-year program there. Morris headed up the first systematic excavations in 1916 when he was twenty-five years old. He established an enviable scientific reputation in regional archeology and was granted the right to live adjacent to the site in a house he constructed using some reclaimed twelfth-century materials from the ruins. He served for a time as the site's first custodian after the National Park Service took over ownership of the property. Later, he returned to Aztec and supervised the reconstruction of the Great Kiva, which stands today as it did eight centuries ago when it was the center of Anasazi ceremonial life.

When American Museum funds for work at Aztec Ruins depleted in the early 1920s, Morris turned to related research across the vast sweeps of the Colorado Plateau. Earlier, he had purchased a 1917 Model T Ford for $104.95. He loaded the open-sided touring car with extra gas and food, a bedroll, water bags, cooking gear, pitch-covered floorboards that could substitute as firewood in barren wastes, and a kit of tools and a shovel to keep the vehicle operating over often-roadless terrain. During the 1930s, Morris's expertise brought him to the Canyon del Muerto, Arizona; the Cliff Place, Mesa Verde, Colorado; and the White House, Canyon de Chelly, Arizona. Upon his death in 1957, his ashes were scattered at the ruins. A bronze plaque in the visitor center there commemorates his contributions to southwestern archeology.

(From *Aztec Ruins National Monument Administrative History of an Archeological Preserve*, Robert H. Lister and Florence C. Lister, National Park Service, 1990.)

THE RUINS
West Ruins

The Animas River was the center of farming for early settlers on the terraced slope of the ruins. Attracted to the valley by its favorable location and fertile irrigatible soil, the site is a more amenable place than the desolate Chaco Canyon and fortress-like galleries of the Mesa Verde tableland. Archeological evidence uncovered by Morris and others suggests that the ruins and mounds visible today result from two construction periods. Tree-ring dating indicates that the multistoried pueblo of the West Ruins was constructed between A.D. 1106 and 1124, with the major construction period between 1111 and 1115.

Morris concluded that this first construction period was built in typical Chaco-style architecture, which was confirmed by Chaco-like pottery and artifacts found at the site. A second major construction period by Mesa Verde–type people occurred between A.D. 1220 and 1250. Remodeling the pueblo and building what is now the east ruin, the newcomers introduced T-shaped doorways and variations on kiva styles, leaving behind pottery, beadwork, and textiles.

There is speculation about an interim dormancy of around 100 years, based on archeological evidence. Whatever the case, construc-

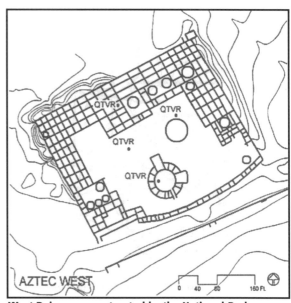

West Ruin as reconstructed by the National Park Service from excavations.

tion techniques and pottery remnants indicate the presence of the Chaco and Mesa Verde cultures on the site. The architecture of the early builders of the West Ruins pueblo closely follows the Chacoan practice of building hundreds of rooms on multiple levels; kivas for ceremonial purposes are integrated into the room layout and stand separately in a plaza. The rooms were laid out in rows adjoining one another—as one row was finished, another was added alongside it.

When several rows were completed, second and possibly third stories were added. A fourth story may have been added in some places.

The size, unity, and elegance of design of the West Ruins provide an interesting visitor's experience. The Chacoan's achievement in community planning and sensitivity to design is seen in their pueblo dwellings and ceremonial activities. During your visit, you can reflect on the cooperative community living in a compact pueblo site, requiring a form of self-government for a division of labor for building, farming, and hunting, as well as leisure time for arts and crafts.

Excavated rooms and surface evidence indicate that many more rooms existed than the 352 rooms counted today: 221 first-story rooms, 119 second-story rooms, and at least 12 third-story rooms. The only entrance into the pueblo is along the path by which visitors enter the ruins today. Rooms were accessed by ladders from the plaza level or through doorways between rooms. Along the northeastern section's second floor are four special doorways, each placed in the corner of a room so it connects with the adjoining diagonal room. One corner doorway, possibly unique in the Southwest, has a second smaller opening beneath it for access into a first-floor room.

To the northwest of the ruins, less than two miles away, the settlers found an outcropping of sandstone suitable for shaping and hauling to the site. Wall construction is Chacoan core-and-veneer masonry, composed of rubble fill and faced with rectangular blocks. The veneer at Aztec Ruins is alternating courses of large rectangular sandstone blocks, shaped into rectangles by pecking or grinding with small, tightly wedged rocks between the larger stones. A distinctive feature of the West Ruins is two very fine bands of green sandstone blocks that extend horizontally along the pueblo's outer west wall and into several interior rooms of the southwest corner. The walls were originally plastered with layers of adobe. Main beams of pine or juniper—one to one-and-a-half feet in diameter and ten to twelve feet long—roofed the rooms. Laid over these were long poles of juniper or cottonwood. Next came a layer of rush or reed matting, and then a layer of dirt and adobe forming the top of the roof or the floor of the room above when there was more than one story.

In contrast to the Chacoan architecture of the Aztec ruins' first period of construction, the Mesa Verdeans built in a looser, less complex style, remodeling and rebuilding within the pueblo. Their masonry walls of rectangular sandstone blocks and cobblestone walls lack the interest of the Chacoan alternating sandstone-block courses. Large Chaco-type rooms were reduced in size with smaller rooms and lowered ceilings. Older doorways were blocked or shortened and narrowed in the style of the ones at Mesa Verde. In some cases, entire small rooms, complete with ceilings, were built within older rooms.

Great Kiva

Toward the end of their occupation of Aztec Ruins, the Chacoans built the Great Kiva in the pueblo plaza. It was remodeled by the Mesa Verdeans, but used only a short time before being abandoned. Excavated in 1921 and reconstructed in 1934 by Morris, it is the only restored Great Kiva in the Southwest. Although unconventional for National Park Service practices, the total rebuilding met Morris's single-minded goal of creating a clearer idea of how communal kivas looked when they were in use.

The Great Kiva, or "House of the Great Kiva" as Morris called it, is centrally located in the south side of the plaza. Descending into the cool underground interior, with its dark red columns and wainscoting lit by daylight from roof and wall openings, reveals a sophisticated structural accomplishment.

The kiva is an underground structure of two concentric circles. The inner part of approximately forty-eight feet in diameter—the kiva proper—has a floor about eight feet below the surface. Two concentric benches three feet high completely encircle the kiva base. At ground level and surrounding this inner section is an outer circle of fourteen pie-shaped rooms. Twelve of these are essentially similar, but the other two are markedly different. One is merely an open passage about three-and-a-half feet wide that leads directly from the plaza to the head of the south stairway. The other is a large rectangular alcove-like structure on the north side of the kiva proper, with a stairway leading up into it from the kiva floor. On the north and west sides of this alcove, there is a low bench-like structure around the inner wall. Toward the center back portion of the alcove is another low, square masonry structure that may have been an altar. For the convenience of visitors, the National Park Service has placed modern wooden stairways at both of these points.

On the kiva's floor are remains of the central altar or fire pit, flanked on either side by two large rectangular stone-lined pits, the bottoms of which are well below the kiva floor. These pits, often referred to as foot drums, may have served at other times as hiding places for the shamans, or medicine men, who performed mystical rites during ceremonies.

Morris concluded that the Great Kiva was originally roofed, after finding the remains of four columns, each three feet square and an estimated eighteen feet high. Each column stood on a stack of four thick, circular sandstone slabs, each three feet in diameter. Composed of alternating courses of masonry and wooden poles, the columns were countersunk below the level of the kiva floor (one column is left exposed to demonstrate the construction method). The weight of the slabs, columns, and roof was spread on a foundation base of cobblestone and sandstone in adobe.

The placement of the pillars in a square in the outer circumference of the kiva precluded a cribbed superstructure such as those on smaller clan, or residential, kivas. From the pattern of burned ceiling residue recovered on the kiva floor, Morris theorized that there were radiating logs extending like spokes of a wheel from this central square to the outside walls of the surface rooms. Over this framework, shorter lengths of timbers were spaced in a cross pattern. As in domestic ceilings, these were covered with shredded cedar bark and a foot of tamped earth. Evidently the kiva burned and was then abandoned.

Visitor Center

The visitor center harbors within its walls the original Morris home. Morris designed and supervised construction of the original house in the Chaco style; it was completed in 1919 and occupied by the archeologist until 1933. Constructed of unplastered masonry walls of salvaged stones, aged beams, and roof poles from the West Ruins to simulate the weathered portion of the ruin, the four-room house with an unfinished exhibit room had a distinctive Southwest pueblo flavor: a living room corner fireplace, tribal rug wall coverings, and cases of pottery and baskets. Exterior touches unique to the ruins were the porch and its cedar posts placed upside down so that the roots

The Earl Morris house about 1933. Today, it houses the Aztec Ruins Visitor Center.

embraced the ends of the roof's cross-beams and crenellated masonry parapets.

In 1925, the exhibit room and a separate comfort station were completed, providing visitor services and museum space until the 1930s. A Public Works Administration (PWA) project completed in 1935 altered the vacated five-room, Morris-house floor plan and exterior to expand visitor services and museum space. A new lobby connected the house and comfort station, a 1,305-square-foot museum was added on the west side of the old house, and a new porch extended across the front of the lobby. The crenellated roofline was modified and the exterior covered in adobe. During Mission 66, in 1958, the museum was expanded to the east by adding restrooms and a workroom. The addition of a collection room in 1984 and wheelchair-accessible restrooms in 1988 completed the present visitor center.

When Morris first undertook the excavations at Aztec, it was his intention, and that of the American Museum of Natural History, to completely uncover the ruins. The massive nature of the undertaking, the intervention of World War I, and a shortage of funds curtailed those ambitious plans. Toward the end of his excavations, Morris realized there was an advantage to leaving parts of any ruin unexcavated to benefit from better future archeological techniques. Except for stabilization work, the National Park Service feels the same way, and they are content to leave the partially excavated and stabilized ruins as seen today.

BANDELIER

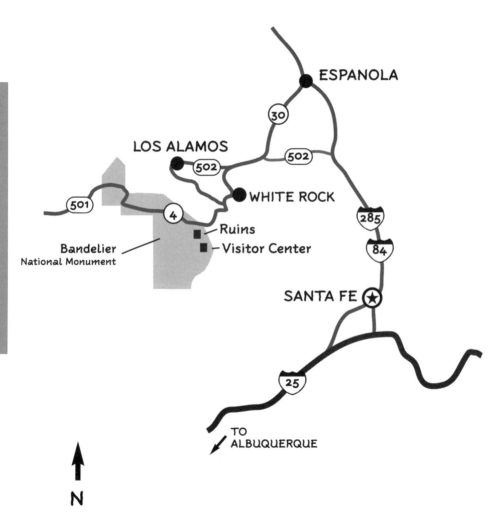

NEW MEXICO

ESPANOLA

30

LOS ALAMOS
502

502

WHITE ROCK

501

4

285

Ruins

Visitor Center

84

Bandelier
National Monument

SANTA FE ★

25

TO
ALBUQUERQUE

N

2

Bandelier
National Monument

Near Los Alamos, Sandoval County, New Mexico
www.nps.gov/band

Bandelier National Monument is 48 miles by road northwest of Santa Fe, New Mexico. From Santa Fe, travel north on U.S. 84/285 to Pojoaque, then west on NM 4 and continue 24 miles to the visitor center.

"The grandest thing I ever saw."

Adolph Bandelier, journal entry, October 23, 1880

Located in the dramatic landscape of the Pajarito Plateau of the Jemez Mountains in north-central New Mexico, Bandelier National Monument has the unique distinction of being a combination of ancestral pueblo dwelling ruins and a superb National Park Service complex—the Bandelier Civil Conservation Corps (CCC) Historic District—built in the 1930s. Prehistoric settlement from the twelfth to sixteenth centuries is visible in the hundreds of ruins of masonry structures and cave shelters in Frijoles and in other canyons and mesas throughout Bandelier. The CCC Historic District is a highly refined design of thirty-one Pueblo Revival buildings and is the largest unaltered collection of such structures in any national park.

Named after Adolph F. A. Bandelier, the monument was established in 1916 and contains 32,737 acres, almost 70 percent of which is designated as wilderness area. The main concentration of Frijoles Canyon ruins is seen from a paved 1.4-mile Main Loop Trail and can be walked in about an hour. Beyond the visitor center, seventy miles of trails radiate out into the terrain of breathtaking beauty—spectacular gorges, erosion-pocked cliffs and canyons, forested mesas, and tumbling waterfalls.

BANDELIER

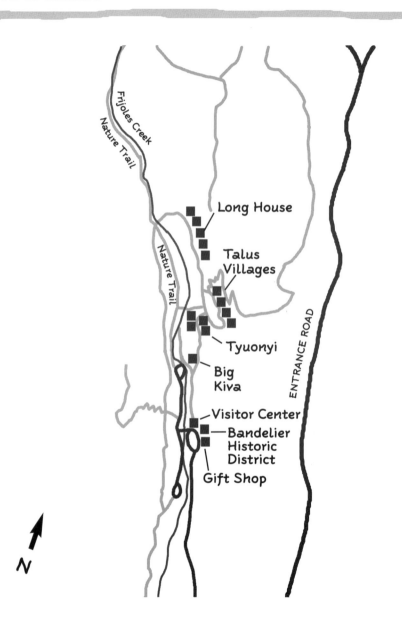

Frijoles Creek

Nature Trail

Nature Trail

Long House

Talus Villages

Tyuonyi

ENTRANCE ROAD

Big Kiva

Visitor Center

Bandelier Historic District

Gift Shop

N

Bandelier ruins.

THE RUINS

Startling geologic events created the dramatic landscape of northwestern New Mexico's Jemez Mountains. Volcanic activity, shaping the Pajarito Plateau and Rio Grande River, also carved Frijoles Creek, which drains into the Rio Grande River. The volcanic ash settling on the plateau formed a rock, softer and lighter than basalt, which created the distinctive pink, beige, and white cliffs of Bandelier. The rock, called tuff, made the digging of homesites in the canyon a simple task.

Bandelier's canyons and mesas contain hundreds of masonry ruins and cave shelters. There is prehistoric evidence of Archaic Indians in the region from around 2000 B.C. Early in the twelfth century, the Anasazi Indians left their original settlements to the north, where they had lived during the ninth to thirteenth centuries, and a group moved toward the upper Rio Grande area west of Santa Fe. The Rio Grande Anasazi settled into the canyon-slashed slopes of the Pajarito Plateau, and for the next three centuries they built villages in the cliffs of the deep gorges and on the valley floor.

El Rito de los Frijoles ("Bean Creek," in Spanish) is an oasis in the dry country of New Mexico. Extending for approximately two miles on the Frijoles Canyon valley floor and carved into cliff walls of compressed volcanic ash are the ruins of kivas, pueblos, masonry houses, and cave rooms. The monument's Main Loop Trail leads past an excavated kiva, the ruins of a large circular pueblo, and talus villages.

Adolph F. A. Bandelier

A Swiss-born self-taught anthropologist-historian, Adolph F. A. Bandelier was a pioneer of modern Southwest archeology. Born in Berne in 1840, Bandelier arrived in Highland, Illinois, at age eight. After law studies in Switzerland, he returned to Highland, married, became active in community affairs, and settled into a banking career. Disenchanted with his life, he was prompted by a fascination with natural history and ancient societies to apply for a grant for a one-man expedition to the Southwest from the Archeological Institute of America. He received the grant.

Thus, at age forty he arrived in Santa Fe in the summer of 1880 to trace the social organization, customs, and movements of southwestern and Mexican peoples. His fieldwork took him to modern-day Cochiti Pueblo and Santo Domingo Pueblo, and finally to the canyon of El Rito de los Frijoles. There, with a feverish excitement, he wandered the canyons and mesas, sketched the ruins, and recorded impressions in his journal. Although he did no excavating, he measured mounds and caves, and collected artifacts and shipped them back to his sponsors in New York City. In eighteen months, Bandelier visited 166 ruins in New Mexico, Arizona, Mexico, Bolivia, and Peru. He returned to the canyon that bears his name only four times after the historic trip in 1880.

The canyon and its ruins captured Bandelier's imagination, and in his 1890 novel *The Delight Makers*, he depicted Pueblo life in pre-Spanish times. In his seventies, he went to Seville, Spain, to study early Spanish records of the Americas. He died there in 1914.

Big Kiva

The excavated and stabilized Big Kiva, the remains of a circular underground structure used for ceremonial purposes, is forty-two feet in diameter and eight feet deep. Originally, it was framed by timber columns and a roof of log beams covered with earth; fire pits, a ventilator shaft, and *sipapu*—a hole in the floor for ancestors' entry into the world—are visible today. In its present and partially restored state, this kiva shows the butt ends of six roof columns similar to those that once bore the load of the roof, as well as the stub ends of roof stringers. The CCC, responsible for much valuable work in the monument during the late 1930s, accomplished the restoration work in this kiva.

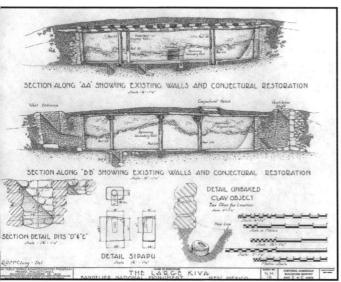

Big Kiva at Bandelier. Drawn by R. P. McLung, Historic American Building Survey, 1939.

Tyuonyi

On the floor of Frijoles Canyon, a little upstream from the visitor center, is Tyuonyi, the chief building of the area, and one of the most impressive pueblo ruins in the Rio Grande drainage area. Situated on a level bench of open ground, perhaps one hundred feet from the Rito Frijoles and fifteen feet above the water, Tyuonyi at one time contained more than four hundred rooms made of blocks of the volcanic tuff that forms the crust of the Pajarito Plateau. This isolated, freestanding circular pueblo, excavated by Edgar L. Hewett in the early 1900s, once stood three stories high in places. Built around a central plaza with three kivas, the pueblo was completely enclosed except for a narrow entryway. The only access to the central plaza and the village was by way of a single narrow passageway on the eastern side of the village, other than by ladders across the rooftops. Its modern aspect is greatly reduced in height; although excavated, no walls have been restored, so that only the ground floor is still evident, with outer and inner walls standing to a height of four or five feet throughout.

Cavate dwelling.

To appreciate the size and layout of Tyuonyi, the visitor should climb the nearby slope until a bird's-eye view reveals the entire ground plan of the huge circle. From above, more than 250 cell-like rooms can be counted, placed in concentric rows around the central plaza. The most massive part of the circle is eight rooms across, narrowing to four rooms in breadth at the brook side. The two- and three-story parts of the building, as computed from the height of the original rubble, were at the massive eastern side. Tree-ring dating has fairly well established the age of the Tyuonyi construction as between A.D. 1383 and 1466, a major building period in the canyon.

Talus Villages

Further along the trail, talus villages—terraced masonry pueblos composed of cave rooms, which were supplemented by at least as many masonry rooms at the front—are set against the base of a vertical cliff where the talus slope meets the valley floor. Dwelling rooms and kivas were built of blocks of tuff carved from the cliffs and logs carried from nearby forested mesas. Floor and roof beams *(vigas)* rested in the holes poked into the soft tufa above and below the caves. Visitors can enter some of these carved-out chambers by ladder. Restoration work done by the Museum of New Mexico in 1920 on the old foundations, with new ceiling beams placed in the ancient holes in the cliff, serves to show faithfully the original appearance of this typical specimen of a talus house. The rooms are small by modern standards, with doors only large enough to squeeze through and no windows.

Long House

About one-fourth of a mile up the canyon from Tyuonyi, also against the northern and sun-warmed 150-foot-high cliff, is the ruin of one of the largest combination cave-and-masonry dwellings to be found anywhere on the plateau. This great ruin is known as Long House for an obvious reason: it stretches out almost eight hundred feet in a continuous block of two or three rooms extending from the rock of the wall face, with hand-carved caves as back rooms. Into this cliff are dug many cave rooms, several kivas, and a variety of storage niches, all of which were incorporated into a single dwelling of more than three hundred rooms rising three stories high. At Long House the rows of *viga* holes in the cliff are particularly conspicuous, defining the one-time roof levels for hundreds of feet at a stretch.

Bandelier Civilian Conservation Corps Historic District

The National Historic Landmark nomination by National Park Service historian Laura Soullière Harrison for Bandelier Civilian Conservation Corps Historic District described the complex in the following way:

Bandelier Civil Conservation Corps Historic District from the mesa, showing the overall design planned around a plaza.

"The exceptional significance of the Bandelier buildings lies in their impact as a group. . . . Taken individually, each structure was a well-detailed, solid piece of work. Collectively, the development was a masterpiece combining fine architecture, landscape architecture, and arts and crafts. The unity of design threaded through the landscaping to the buildings and their contents . . . and created a sense of place so strong that it predominates today. The whole is greater than the sum of the parts."

Despite difficult access from the mesa down to the Rito Frijoles, a small dude ranch had been built in 1907 and was expanded by George and Evelyn Frey when they purchased the property in 1925. There was no road into the canyon in the monument's early years. Supplies were lowered from the mesa by a tramway, and visitors either rode horseback or hiked down a steep trail to the canyon floor. When National Park Service director Horace Albright wanted to expand the national park system, he succeeded in having Bandelier transferred from Forest Service jurisdiction to the National Park Service by presidential proclamation in 1932. Bandelier retained its national monument status but was enlarged to include additional ruins. The process of protecting the ruins, improving access, and creating visitor services was assigned to the Southwestern Monuments unit of the National Park Service.

The National Park Service Branch of Plans and Design, whose architects and landscape architects worked under the direction of Thomas C. Vint, designed the Frijoles Canyon development of twenty-nine Pueblo Revival–style buildings (two additional buildings are outside the canyon) as the administrative, visitor service, and maintenance core of Bandelier National Monument. Construction by CCC members began in 1935 and was completed in 1941. The adobe-washed tufa-block building group is the largest unaltered collection of such structures in the national park system and is suitably designated a National Historic Landmark.

Entryway to lodge courtyards.

The building group provided a complete development for the national monument: visitor services, lodging for guests, and office space and residences for employees. Lodging was necessary because the nearest accommodations were in Santa Fe, reached in the 1930s by eighteen miles of rough dirt road and seventeen miles of partially paved highway. The design concept, construction program, and finished architecture represent a fascinating episode in the creation of a cohesive complex of distinctive and exceptional Pueblo Revival design.

The Frijoles Canyon development was conceived as a building group wrapped around three sides of a central parking plaza. Administrative offices are at one end, the walls of the maintenance yard at the other end, and the buildings of the newer Frijoles Canyon Lodge on a connecting side. (The lodge is no longer in service.) The fourth side is bordered by the Rito Frijoles. The two main plaza façades are the lodge lobby and dining room, and the headquarters/museum building. The individual guest lodges were reached by a series of flagstone pathways that led up from the lodge lobby through small courtyards and patios that stepped up the hillside on several levels. Outdoor areas were planted with native vegetation. A separate complex of employee residences was placed up the hillside from the entrance road, concealed from visitor view by vegetation and the terrain.

The designers used locally available building materials, and the adobe-washed tufa-block structures reflect local cultural traditions in scale, color, texture, and massing. Handmade furniture and light fixtures grace the interiors. From the flat canyon floor to the steeper terrain toward the base of the cliff, the existing topography was respected by constructing buildings on several elevations, as reflected in the stepped-roof parapets. Landscape planning contributed to the final effect, including blasted rocks along the entrance road, stained for a weathered appearance.

The ingenuity of the designers and managers was severely tested by the

Wall surfaces are completely plastered and vigas and canales project from the roofline below parapets.

funding constraints of the Emergency Construction Works program, which had a statutory limit of $1,500 on materials for any one building constructed in a national park and a limit of six months for workers' enrollment in the CCC, although workers could and often did reenlist. The solution that successfully overcame this challenge was the decision to design and build in a modular manner. By building many small projects and connecting them with portals, courtyards, and walls, the architects devised a cohesive and pleasing development on a very human scale. The individual buildings are tied together by a series of stone walls, plastered portals, flagstone walkways, and stone-edged planting beds. The consistent use of stone and mud-plastered walls gives a strong sense of unity. The interplay of mass and void, as when a solid building face is relieved by a recessed portal, adds spatial diversity.

National Park Service architect Lyle Bennett supervised the overall landscape design and the majority of the building designs. His supervision ensured continuity; everything was designed and constructed with similar architectural elements and materials. Stone, timber, gravel, clay, and sand came from the site or the nearby Santa Fe National Forest. The basic building material was stone cut from the local rhyolite tuff. The soft stone could be rough cut at the quarry and later finished at a building site.

All interiors followed Spanish Colonial and Pueblo Revival themes. Wall surfaces were finished with hard plaster and were often painted with Spanish Colonial and Indian motifs. Most ceilings were exposed *vigas* supporting aspen *latillas*, sometimes in herringbone patterns. Traditional corner fireplaces built of tuff and firebrick were placed in many rooms. Interior woodwork was frequently carved in decorative patterns developed specifically for the project by the designers. Typical floors were flagstone, varnished to a high glossy finish. The additive quality of the Pueblo Revival style was expressed by a one- or two-step change in levels between rooms.

The overall unity of the design was completed with a Spanish Colonial theme incorporated into the lodge furniture and light fixtures, designed by National Park Service architects and built by CCC craftsmen. Exterior and interior light fixtures, wall switchplates, and mirror frames were cut from tin, scratched, dotted, soldered together, and painted. Federal Arts Project artists Pablita Velarde, Helmut Naumer, Chris Jorgensen, and Raymond Terken all contributed artwork.

The Bandelier project is remarkable for its high-quality craftsmanship. The Frijoles Canyon development employed several thousand people, and everything from stonecutting to interior details and furnishings was executed at a master craftsman level. Unskilled workers were provided with on-the-job training. Using traditional techniques, with tools such as broad axes and adzes, the CCC enrollees did exemplary work. The Bandelier building group is also noteworthy as the largest collection of CCC-built structures in a national park not subsequently diluted by the addition of new buildings.

The choice of Pueblo Revival style for Bandelier fit perfectly with the goal that national park architecture should harmonize with its environment. It expressed the true principles of Rustic architecture as a national movement rather than a local style, one that could embrace any number of regional styles but produced consistently individual structures and enclaves that looked as though they belonged in their setting. The completed complex shows an architectural unity of theory and style that begins with site and building design and continues inside with fine interior details. Collectively, it is a masterpiece combining fine architecture, landscape architecture, and arts and crafts, and is suitably designated as a National Historic Landmark.

CHACO CULTURE

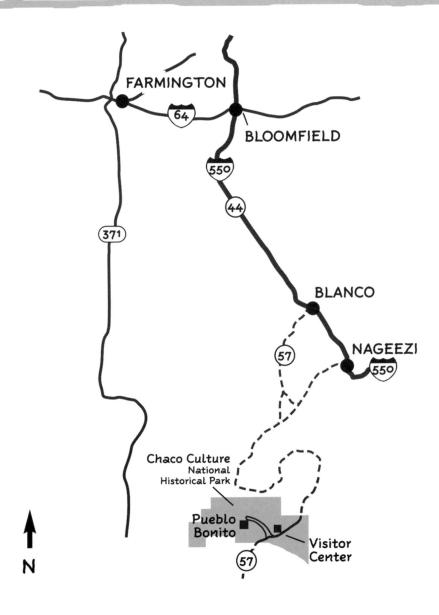

FARMINGTON

64

BLOOMFIELD

550

44

371

BLANCO

57

NAGEEZI

550

NEW MEXICO

Chaco Culture
National
Historical Park

Pueblo
Bonito

Visitor
Center

57

N

3

Chaco Culture
National Historical Park

Nageezi, San Juan County, New Mexico
www.nps.gov/chcu

Chaco Canyon is located in northwestern New Mexico. The preferred and recommended access route to the park is from the north, from U.S. 550 (formerly NM 44). At the Nageezi trading post turn left onto County Road 7900 (paved road) and follow signs 21 miles to the visitor center. From the south, two routes access Chaco from Highway 9. Both routes are infrequently maintained, and they can become impassable during inclement weather.

> ". . . ruin of ruins, the equal of which in point of magnitude and general interest, is not to be found among the world's collection of discovered prehistoric structures."
>
> H. S. Holsinger, *Report on the Prehistoric Ruins of Chaco Canyon, New Mexico, December 18, 1900,* General Land Office, Washington, D.C.

Chaco Culture National Historical Park in northwestern New Mexico preserves one of America's most significant and fascinating cultural and historic areas. From the mid-ninth century to the early twelfth century, Chaco Canyon was the cultural, economic, and political center of the Chaco Anasazi, an Ancestral Pueblo culture. A region-wide system of communities and trade, linked by an elaborate road network, radiated outwards to the prehistoric Four Corners area.

Chaco Canyon seems an unlikely place for a major center of ancestral Puebloan culture to take root and flourish. This remote and seemingly barren mile-and-a-half canyon, with searing heat and a depth of three hundred feet, appears incapable of sustaining a population that influenced a vast region. This

133

CHACO CULTURE

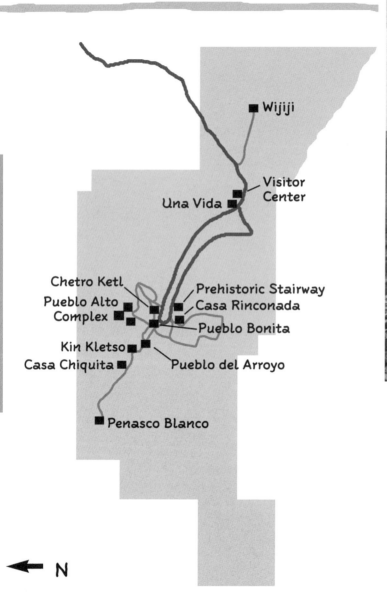

Wijiji

Visitor Center

Una Vida

Chetro Ketl
Prehistoric Stairway
Pueblo Alto Complex
Casa Rinconada
Pueblo Bonita
Kin Kletso
Casa Chiquita
Pueblo del Arroyo

Penasco Blanco

← N

NEW MEXICO

A solitary wall of Una Vida pueblo.

is high desert country, with long winters, short growing seasons, and marginal rainfall—average annual precipitation at Chaco is only eight inches. Chaco Wash bisects the canyon. On the canyon's south side, crumbling cliffs spill fans of broken eroded rock onto the canyon bottom. Unlike the canyon's sloping southern side, the northern canyon walls rise smoothly and abruptly, intersected by smaller canyons carrying runoff from the mesa. Under this sheer, sandstone escarpment, the Chacoans chose to construct their great houses.

Despite the harsh environment, Chaco is remarkable for its monumental public and ceremonial buildings, as well as its distinctive architecture standing against the sheer red-and-ocher sandstone walls of Chaco Canyon, which rise four and five stories high. Today, thirteen major ruins stand along the now-dry Chaco Wash at the bottom of the canyon. Many of the structures have survived the centuries remarkably intact, with original timbers in place. However, you shouldn't be disappointed

at collapsed piles of un-excavated masonry or partially fallen walls. In this remote and inhospitable place, a cultural flowering occurred—the Chaco Phenomenon—marked by well-organized and skillful planning, designing, resource gathering, and construction. The Chacoan people combined architec-

Pueblo Bonito, the largest pueblo in the canyon.

tural designs with consistent use of forms and materials, astronomical alignments, landscaping, irrigation, and engineering to create an ancient urban center of spectacular public architecture—one that still amazes and inspires us a thousand years later.

The lack of written records leaves the history of the Chacoan and Anasazi cultures shrouded in mystery. What happened in Chaco Canyon remains an enigma, although it has been subject to a century of archeological work. Studies have been published on Chacoan planning and architecture, social organization, road systems, trade networks, irrigation systems, ceremonial life, archeoastronomy, and outlying communities (outliers). In 1971, the Chaco Project, under the direction of the National Park Service and in conjunction with the University of New Mexico, applied a full spectrum of refined technologies to solve the mysteries of Chaco Canyon. They applied dendrochronology (tree-ring dating), stratigraphy (examining middens), remote sensing (low-level aerial photography), archeomagnetic dating (magnetic alignments), archeoastronomy, paleobotanical research, carbon-14 dating, and computer modeling. Added to discoveries from pick-and-shovel archeology, a chronology of Chacoan culture fell in place. Although evidence defines the Chaco road network—where it was, how wide, and how it was built—the "why" is subject to much speculation and hypotheses to fill in the unwritten record.

Chaco Canyon National Monument was designated in 1907, and redesignated and renamed Chaco Culture National Historical Park in 1980. The park was expanded from its original 21,512 acres to a total of 33,974 acres to protect thirty-three Anasazi settlements outlying Chaco Canyon, as well as the communities that surround them. In 1987, the park was designated a World Heritage Site.

Chacoan doorways and walls of Pueblo Bonito.

SETTLEMENT HISTORY

The remains of early hunters and farmers in the canyon date back at least 8,500 years. By about A.D. 500, these people began living in aboveground, one-story masonry dwellings built around a central pithouse. The Chaco Phenomenon appeared in the canyon beginning around A.D. 900, seen most clearly in the grand scale of the architecture. The people started building great houses of multiple stories containing hundreds of rooms much larger than any they had previously built. The buildings were planned from the start, in contrast to the usual practice of adding rooms to existing structures as needed. Succeeding generations maintained the form and geometry of the pueblos that started with modest blocks of rooms. Construction on some of these buildings spanned decades and even centuries. Although each is unique, all the great houses share architectural features that make them recognizable as Chacoan: a coherent plan, overall mass of structures (dwellings and ceremonial buildings), distinctive core-and-veneer sandstone masonry walls, enclosed plazas, and the architecture of the kivas.

During the middle and late 800s, the great houses of Pueblo Bonito, Una Vida, and Peñasco Blanco were constructed, followed by Hungo Pavi, Chetro Ketl, Pueblo Alto, Pueblo del Arroyo, Wijiji, Kin Kletso, Casa Chiquita, and others. These structures were often oriented to solar, lunar, and cardinal directions. Lines of sight between the great houses allowed communication. Sophisticated astronomical markers, communication features, water control devices, and formal earthen mounds surrounded them. The buildings were placed within a landscape surrounded by sacred mountains, mesas, and shrines that still have deep spiritual meaning for Native Americans today.

After prevailing for three hundred years, Chaco Canyon declined as a regional center during the middle 1100s, when new construction ceased. For another hundred years, limited renovations and additions were made to the great houses at Chaco. Chacoan influence continued at Aztec Ruins and other centers to the north, south, and west into the late 1100s and 1200s. In time, the people shifted away from Chacoan ways, migrated to new areas, reorganized their own world, and eventually interacted with foreign cultures. Their descendants are likely the modern Southwest Native Americans.

In 1848, the U.S. Army sent Lt. James H. Simpson to survey the new territory of New Mexico. Simpson routinely found ruins and artifacts in his work, but what he discovered in Chaco Canyon was stunning. He found huge three- and four-story houses built with exquisite stonework and containing hundreds of rooms. In an area covering more than thirty square miles, Chaco Canyon revealed nine ancient towns with "Great Houses" and 2,400 archeological sites. So extraordinary was Simpson's find and so perplexing were the unanswered

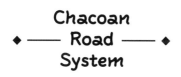

Chacoan Road System

Aerial photographs reveal the ancient Chacoan road system, made up of more than four hundred miles of road connecting Chaco to some seventy-five communities. Hundreds of miles of roads have been associated with the Chacoan culture, including more than half a dozen trade routes. The longest road presently known runs north forty-two miles toward the prehistoric towns now called Salmon Ruins, on the San Juan River, and Aztec Ruins, on the Animas River. On the north-south roads, settlements lay at travel intervals of approximately one day on foot. The roads appear to date from the eleventh and twelfth centuries, a time of expanding population. Several roads converged at Pueblo Alto from the north. From there, well-defined stairways led to the canyon bottom.

These roads were not simply trails worn by centuries of foot travel. They were the productions of relatively sophisticated engineering and required a great deal of energy and thought to plan, construct, and maintain. Laid out in long straight lines with scant regard for terrain, the roads averaged thirty feet in width. Construction was simple. Chacoan road builders scraped off the top layer of soil to expose a harder layer below. The typical subsurface was caliche, formed when naturally occurring calcium carbonate binds sand and other material into a hard, concrete-like substance. On sloping ground, the roadbed was leveled and a rock berm built to retain the fill. Where the roads passed over bare rock, masonry walls or a line of boulders often bordered them.

The road network could have facilitated communications and trade in the Chacoan world. During Classic times, Chaco was the center of a far-flung trading network. Goods were exchanged internally within the Chacoan system and externally with groups as far south as Mexico. Raw turquoise was imported from distant mines and transformed with exquisite craftsmanship into necklaces, bracelets, and pendants. Great quantities of such jewelry have been found here, more than at any other southwestern site. Evidence of pottery made elsewhere, and the many seashells (often strung into necklaces), copper bells, and remains of macaws or parrots found in Chaco Canyon suggest contact with central Mexico, perhaps with the ancient Toltecs.

questions that the curator of the American Museum of Natural History, David Hurst Thomas, referred to it as the Chaco Phenomenon.

STRUCTURES

Eight of the dozen major Chaco Canyon ruins can be reached from the one-way loop road; other sites, such as Peñasco Blanco, Tsin Kletsin, and Pueblo Alto, require some hiking. The appearance and condition of most of the park's exposed ruins and those unexcavated sites with standing walls are due to an intensive stabilization program begun by the National Park Service in 1933. The program undid previous preservation work, and drainage was realigned around the ruins to minimize moisture damage. Stabilization and maintenance is ongoing.

The Chaco Anasazi were skilled masons. Working without metal tools or any formal mathematics, they put up vast communal buildings that still compel admiration. Their methods evolved over centuries. The earliest dwellings were constructed with simple walls, one-stone thick, with generous courses of mud mortar. The oldest walls in Pueblo Bonito used this type of masonry. The last distinctive masonry style, called McElmo, appears in Kin Kletso, a late-eleventh-century dwelling. Its walls were built with a thin inner core of rubble and thick outer veneers of shaped sandstone, somewhat similar to the masonry styles used at Mesa Verde.

When the Chacoans began to build higher and more extensively, they employed walls with thick inner cores of rubble and

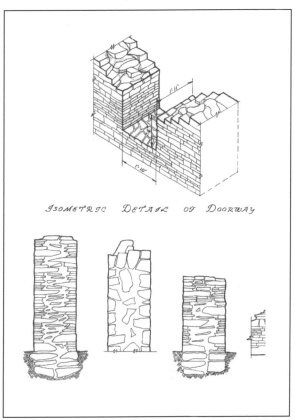

ISOMETRIC DETAIL OF DOORWAY

Evolving types of core-and-veneer walls.

fairly thin veneers of facing stone. The core-and-veneer walls tapered as they rose, evidence of the planning that went into the large-scale construction between A.D. 1000 and 1200. An early example of this type of wall is characterized by large blocks of irregular sandstone chinked with smaller stones set into the mortar.

Una Vida

The pueblo closest to the visitor center, Una Vida, is a short walk from the parking lot. Construction was underway by the mid-900s and continued until late in the mid-1100s, concurrent with construction at Pueblo Bonito and Peñasco Blanco. A semicircular wall connects two wings of the L-shaped pueblo. There are about five kivas and 150 rooms in the structure. Only partially excavated, it is in much the same condition as seen by Lt. James H. Simpson of the U.S. Army. It is an excellent example of a mostly unexcavated site.

Una Vida (meaning "one life" in Spanish) was known to the Navajos as "witchcraft woman's house;" it was associated with a well-known local legend of a witch who held human hostages atop Fajada Butte without food or water. With a floor area of approximately two acres, Una Vida is the fifth-largest pueblo in the Canyon. A long span of construction of any of the Chacoan buildings is established by twenty-nine tree-ring dates ranging from A.D. 847 to 1093. Additional construction in the 1070s added 4,500 square feet of storage space.

Pueblo Bonito

Farther down the canyon, about a half-mile from the visitor center, lies Pueblo Bonito, center of the Chaco world and largest of the pueblos. Pueblo Bonito is the most celebrated and most thoroughly investigated site in Chaco Canyon. Constructed in stages from the mid-800s to the 1200s, Pueblo Bonito (meaning "beautiful town" in Spanish) epitomizes the great pueblo architecture found here and is one of the most extensively excavated and studied sites in North America. Carravahal, a guide from San Juan Pueblo, provided Lt. James Simpson with its name during a military expedition that came through Chaco in 1849. Following the expedition, Simpson published the first detailed description of the ruins in Chaco Canyon.

The immense, D-shaped structure is 520 feet by 310 feet in its outer dimensions and covers more than three acres of ground. The structure rises four or five stories and was honeycombed with more than six hundred rooms. A plaza at the front of the complex is dotted with three large kivas and thirty smaller ones. A one-story row of rooms encloses the pueblo's perimeter.

Archeological work at Pueblo Bonito revealed that the builders had no compunction about filling in and covering over old spaces with new rooms and kivas. The core-and-veneer masonry, with roughly shaped pieces of sandstone laid in mud mortar and faced with carefully selected shaped stones to create the veneer, was rebuilt over and over again. After the walls were built and roofed, a plaster coating was applied over most of the walls that concealed this fine stonework, protecting the mud mortar from rain. The walls of many interior plaster-covered walls were covered with bands of color, usually red or white, but occasionally turquoise.

The pueblo was stepped so that each story opened onto a terrace formed by the roof of the story below. Ladders of poles lashed together provided access to upper levels and down into circular kivas. Rooms that faced onto the terraces contained tools and furnishings, while the dark, often featureless rooms behind were used for storerooms.

The rock for construction was quarried from dense dark sandstone on the cliffs just behind the great Chacoan houses. Once quarried, it was probably dropped to the canyon floor, where it was shaped and dressed. The Anasazi builders chose Pueblo Bonito's location even though they would have recognized the threat of a rock fall from the cliff face to the north. National Park Service engineers fruitlessly attempted to prevent Threatening Rock from splintering away from the cliff's face. They built a supporting masonry terrace below, which slowed the erosion of soil from below the rock, delaying its collapse. It took eight centuries for the enormous block of sandstone's estimated 30,000 tons to collapse in 1941, crushing part of the pueblo's north wall and all or part of sixty-five rooms.

Chetro Ketl

One of the largest Chacoan villages, Chetro Ketl is located about one-quarter mile southeast of Pueblo Bonito. It was built in stages; tree-ring and stratigraphy dating places the first construction period from A.D. 945 to 1030. Chetro Ketl experienced a second major construction phase from 1030 to 1090 when it was remodeled and enlarged, and the core-and-veneer masonry style was further refined. A third and last construction period of a brief eighteen years ended in 1117. Chetro Ketl flourished for about 175 years, then all building ceased.

Like Pueblo Bonito, the walls of the D-shaped structure are about five stories high. Distinctive for its two elevated kivas and artificially raised plaza about twelve feet above the surrounding landscape, Chetro Ketl contained more than five hundred rooms and sixteen kivas. The remains of a colonnade (later filled in during remodeling) along the rear wall of the plaza suggest influences from Mexico. In the cliffs behind the ruin are ancient stairways that lead to prehistoric roadways connecting Chetro Ketl to Pueblo Alto and other outlying communities.

Along the inside of the five-hundred-foot-long rear wall are long rows of room blocks. Excavations revealed that the courtyard is underlaid with kivas of all sizes from earlier periods of construction. Some of the lower rooms were filled in or used for storage, while the upper rooms, many of them terraced, were living quarters. The thick, core-and-veneer masonry walls were faced with a veneer of Chacoan banded masonry. The veneer consisted of rows of larger stone blocks alternating with several rows of smaller tablet-shaped stone layers to form banded patterns that varied with each new construction period or remodeling.

Pueblo del Arroyo

Pueblo del Arroyo (meaning "village by the stream" in Spanish), located just above the modern channel of the Chaco Wash, was built in stages over a relatively short time. The central part was started about A.D 1075; north and south wings were added between 1101 and 1105. The D-shaped pueblo that rose three and four stories in the rear, stepping down to one story in front, had about 280 rooms and more than twenty kivas.

Pueblo del Arroyo's most unique feature is a structure abutting the rear wall. This Tri-Wall structure—an enclosure of three concentric circular walls—has a single tree-ring date of 1109. Exceptional for Chaco Canyon, the structure is similar to a handful of other Anasazi ruins in the Southwest.

Kin Kletso and Casa Chiquita

Kin Kletso and Casa Chiquita seem to have been constructed in the early twelfth century, near the end of Chaco's monumental construction. In the evolution of building in the canyon, the last arrivals were the McElmo Phase, people who came to Chaco from the northern San Juan region of Mesa Verde and Montezuma Valley. Architecture of more compact pueblos of a masonry style, similar to the Mesa Verdean region, differed from earlier Chacoan great houses. The walls were made of large shaped blocks quarried from the softer sandstone near the base of the cliffs and laid two or more rows thick. Rooms and kivas fit into a compact rectilinear structure without an enclosed plaza.

Kin Kletso (meaning "yellow house" in Navajo) is a rectangular, medium-sized pueblo at the foot of the cliff about a half mile northwest of Pueblo Bonito.

This pueblo had about one hundred rooms—around fifty-five ground-level rooms, four kivas, and a tower kiva. The pueblo, which reached at least two stories high, was excavated in the early 1950s.

Casa Rinconada

On the south side of the Chaco Wash is the great kiva known as Casa Rinconada (meaning "cornered house" or "house where the canyon meets" in Spanish). The kiva is the largest in the park and one of the largest in the Southwest. Surrounded by a cluster of excavated fifty-room villages and almost directly across from Pueblo Bonito, this kiva may have served as a ceremonial center for the community at large.

Similar to the great kivas at Pueblo Bonito and Chetro Ketl, Casa Rinconada is a double-walled kiva, or ceremonial room. The kiva is over eighty feet in diameter with walls thirty inches thick—the outer wall is eight feet from the inner wall, the space between being divided into rooms with small rectangular openings. A masonry bench circles the inner walls; above the bench are twenty-eight spaced niches and six larger, less regularly spaced wall crypts. The reconstructed kiva at Aztec Ruins National Monument illustrates the standard features of a great kiva: a firebox, floor vaults, a north stairway entrance with antechambers, and stone-lined pits that held enormous timbers supporting the roof.

Most great kivas, including Casa Rinconada, are precisely aligned on a north-south axis established by the line connecting the centers of the north and south doorways, which has an azimuth of 359°56'.

Other Chaco Canyon Pueblos

Hiking trails lead to a number of other canyon sites. Pueblo Alto, on top of the mesa, is important as the junction of several prehistoric roads. Kin Kletso and Peñasco Blanco can be reached by hiking from the central canyon. Wijiji, built in a single stage in the early 1100s, is notable for its symmetrical layout and rooms of uniform size. Hiking permits are required for these trails and can be obtained at the visitor center.

COLLECTIONS

A new museum in the visitor center has artifacts excavated from the site, including pottery painted with a characteristic black-and-white geometric design, cooking and eating utensils, sandals, spearheads, turquoise jewelry, and copper bells from Mexico. The Museum of New Mexico in Santa Fe and the Maxwell Museum of Anthropology at the University of New Mexico in Albuquerque have collections from their Chaco investigations. Most artifacts and records assembled by various National Park Service activities are housed in the Chaco Center in Albuquerque. The American Museum of Natural History in New York City retains most of the artifacts from the hugely successful 1900 Hyde Exploring Expedition, which shipped three railroad-boxcar loads of excavated objects from Pueblo Bonito to the museum. Other early artifacts held by sponsoring organizations include the U.S. National Museum and the National Geographic Society.

FORT UNION

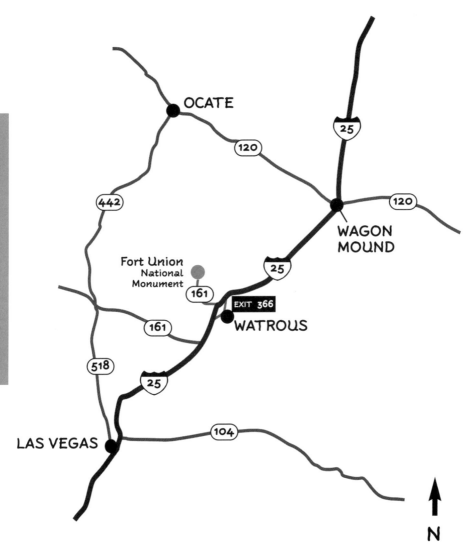

OCATE

120

25

442

120

WAGON
MOUND

Fort Union
National
Monument

25

161

EXIT 366

161

WATROUS

518

25

LAS VEGAS

104

N

NEW MEXICO

4

Fort Union
National Monument

Near Watrous, Mora County, New Mexico
www.nps.gov/foun

Travelers on I-25 should take exit 366. Follow the signs to Fort Union National Monument, which is 8 miles off the interstate on NM Highway 161.

> "The ruins of Fort Union graphically commemorate the achievements of the men who won the West. Located on the route of the Santa Fe Trail where mountains meet the plains, the fort is centered in a region of historic events and brimming with the romance of the frontier."
>
> Robert M. Utley, *Fort Union National Monument*, National Park Service Handbook Number 35, 1962

The barren plains in northeastern New Mexico, once crossed by the Santa Fe Trail, is the site of Fort Union National Monument. Once the commercial artery between the United States and Santa Fe, and later the route of migrants, the trail became legendary in American folklore. In 1851, following the 1846–48 Mexican-American War, which won New Mexico for the United States, a fort was established at the junction of the Mountain and Cimarron Cutoff Branches to protect travelers on the trail and local residents from Indian attacks, as well as to provide a headquarters for the military department of New Mexico.

As a military post to protect travel and settlement, Fort Union played a key role in shaping the destiny of the Southwest for forty years. During the first decade of its existence, the fort stood as the guardian of the Santa Fe Trail, acting as a federal presence in the Territory of New Mexico. The Civil War added to the fort's fame at the battle of Glorietta Pass, where Union soldiers stopped the invading Southern columns. Three different forts were constructed close together at this strategically important site. The third and final Fort Union, whose ruins you see today, functioned as a military garrison, territorial arsenal, and military supply depot for the Southwest. Abandoned by the Army in 1891, the 720-acre site was designated a national monument in 1954.

Today, it is difficult to look at the remnants of limestone foundations, adobe walls, and the few chimneys that rise above the plains and realize that this was once the largest U.S. military installation on the nineteenth-century southwestern frontier. A self-guided tour, starting from the visitor center that contains exhibits of military life in the fort, leads through the ruins of the third fort, the remains of the second fort erected during the Civil War, and a network of ruts along the Santa Fe Trail. During the summer, history talks and demonstrations are offered on weekends.

The ruins of Fort Union—which was once the largest U.S. military installation on the nineteenth-century southwestern frontier—are preserved as an outdoor museum.

DEFENDING THE SOUTHWEST

Following the end of the Mexican-American War in 1848, scattered small units of soldiers served in the Territory of New Mexico to protect settlers and travel routes. This arrangement proved unsatisfactory, and in April 1851, Lt. Col. Edwin V. Sumner, who was commanding Military Department No. 9, which included the New Mexico territory, was ordered "to revise the whole system of defense" for the entire territory. Sumner moved quickly, consolidating the small garrisons and relocating them closer to the Indian country. His first action after taking command was to move his headquarters and supply depot one hundred miles west of Santa Fe to a site strategically located at the junction of the Mountain and Cimarron Cutoff Branches of the Santa Fe Trail.

Remembering the location from earlier campaigns in the area, Sumner chose a place next to a spring beneath a piñon-forested mesa. In August 1851, troops began building the first of three forts in the valley. The unskilled labor erected a garrison of thirty or more log-and-earth structures that were constantly in need of repair. For a decade, the fort served as the base for military operations and as a key station on the Santa Fe Trail. It also served as the principal quartermaster depot of the Southwest. Most traces of the fort, a mile west of the monument, have vanished and the area is not open to the public. The ruins there today are those of the Fort Union Ordnance Depot constructed in the 1860s.

When the Civil War broke out in 1861, the majority of officers at Fort Union joined the South (including the last prewar commander of the fort, Maj. Henry H. Sibley), while most of the regular troops were reassigned to Union forces in the East. Under the new commander of New Mexico operations, Col. Edward R. S. Canby, volunteer regiment replacements from California and Colorado took over guarding the frontier. Concerned that a Confederate invasion would attempt to take over the territory and seize mineral resources of Colorado and an outlet to California, Canby ordered a second fort designed to block the Santa Fe Trail.

A massive earthwork defensive fortification—known as the Star Fort—was started in July 1861. Badly sited against artillery fire from the mesa, the unsodded parapets soon eroded into the surrounding ditch and unbarked pine logs quickly rotted. Built partly underground, the rooms were damp, unventilated, and, consequently, unhealthy. Rather than live in the hovels, most of the troops slept in tents outside the fort.

In early 1862, the Confederates under Gen. Sibley forced Union troops to evacuate Star Fort. At this crucial moment, the first Colorado Volunteer regiment, led by Col. John P. Slough, arrived in New Mexico. Between the opposing forces lay Glorietta Pass—twenty miles southeast of Santa Fe—a rugged opening

The ◆ ── Santa Fe ── ◆ Trail

The 1821 revolution that freed Mexico from Spain opened the way to Santa Fe for American traders. An enterprising Missourian, William Bicknell, lashed trade goods to mules and headed west. By the end of the decade, caravans annually pushed west from the Missouri River. In 1825, the federal government sent George C. Sibley to survey a suitable route for the traders. The wagon masters often went their own way, finding the shortest routes through the unbroken prairie sod. Wagon wheel ruts cut deeply into the sod, broadening into a trough often several hundred yards wide that is still visible today along stretches of grassland in Kansas, Oklahoma, and New Mexico.

The trail began on the west bank of the Missouri River, first at Franklin, then at Independence, and later at Westport. Filled with hardship and danger, the eight-hundred-mile journey to Santa Fe took about two months. Weather could shift from scorching winds whipping across the prairies, to drenching rain turning the trail into a muddy quagmire, to clouds of dust hanging heavy on the wagon trains, burning the travelers' eyes and caking their throats. Wagons bounced along rutted traces, damaging cargo and wagon alike, and the wagon wheels dried and shrank, making constant repairs necessary.

People starting at Independence, Missouri, usually rendezvoused at Council Groves, Kansas. The Trail forked at Fort Dodge, one route continuing west into Colorado and then turning south at Bent's Old Fort, and the other going southwest through the Cimarron Desert. Both branches merged at Fort Union, seventy-five miles from Santa Fe. The Cimarron route was the shorter and more dangerous because of infrequent waterholes and hostile Indians. But if a wagon train made it through the desert and avoided the Indians, a trader could beat his rivals to Santa Fe and reap the first and largest profits.

From 1821 until 1879, when the railroad reached Las Vegas, New Mexico, the Santa Fe Trail served as one of the West's great routes for freight wagons, emigrant caravans, stagecoaches, and military columns. As such, it established a place in American history that helped tie the Southwest to the rest of the country.

through the Sangre de Cristo Mountains. On March 28, 1862, the two armies fought the decisive battle of the Civil War in the far western theater. In three days Union troops had achieved a victory, effectively ending the Confederate threat in the Southwest. The second fort was abandoned after the Confederates withdrew to Texas. In November 1862, the new departmental commander, Brig. Gen. James H. Carleton, gave orders to begin work on the third and final Fort Union, adjacent to Star Fort.

The sprawling installation, erected between 1863 and 1869 by several hundred civilians and modified somewhat in the 1870s, was the most extensive in the territory. It consisted of the military post of Fort Union, with all its attendant structures and a hospital; the Fort Union Quartermaster Depot, with warehouses, corrals, shops, offices, and quarters; and the Fort Union Ordnance Depot. The Post and Quartermaster Depot were built next to each other on the valley floor northeast of the Star Fort. The Ordnance Depot rose on the site of the old log fort at the western edge of the valley.

Star Fort and the Third Fort Union.

The fort served as the central supply base for the army in the West, which attempted to control raids and other hostilities by Apaches, Arapahoes, Cheyennes, Comanches, Kiowas, and Navajos. The Plains Indian threat finally came to a conclusion in 1875 after a successful campaign against the tribes called the Red River War. The decline of the fort and depot began when the first locomotive of the Atchison, Topeka & Santa Fe Railroad steamed into Las Vegas, New Mexico, on Independence Day 1879. The fort survived another eleven years, albeit reduced to a caretaker status.

In 1890, with the census reports' symbolic closing of the Frontier, the War Department decided to abandon many of the old frontier posts, including Fort Union. As a result, Fort Union was officially closed a year later. On February 21, 1891, singing "There's a Land that is Fairer than This," the Tenth Infantry marched out from Fort Union for good. One noncommissioned person stayed as a caretaker. Three years later, the War Department relinquished claim to the land on which Fort Union stood. Finally, both the land and title reverted to the original owners of the Mora Land Grant.

THE FORT STRUCTURES

The third and final fort's buildings were a sharp contrast to its short-lived predecessors. Fort Union Post and Fort Union Quartermaster Depot were roughly four large rectangles in plan, two each for the post and depot. Built in the Territorial style of architecture that came to be associated with New Mexico, they were simple, functional rectangles adorned with brick copings and white-painted doorways and window openings. Officers' quarters were distinctive, with columned porticos across the front of the building. Materials of local origin were used in stone foundations and walls of adobe brick, molded from soil dug from the valley north of the fort and coated with plaster fired in lime kilns south of the fort. Wall copings and chimneys were made of bricks manufactured in Las Vegas, New Mexico. Some items—tools, nails, window glass, fire bricks, and roofing tin—were hauled over the Santa Fe Trail from Fort Leavenworth, Kansas. Water for all three units of the fort came from wells and storage cisterns spotted among the buildings. All the buildings were heated by fireplaces and lighted by spacious windows by day and candles or oil lamps by night.

Post Structures

The nearest structures to the visitor center on the self-guided walking tour are the post structures, beginning with the officers' quarters and company quarters facing the parade ground and flagpole. The nine houses that made up officers' row

Officers Quarters, Fort Union, N. M.

Fort Union Officers' Quarters in 1875.

lined the west side of a spacious parade ground. In the center of the line stood the home of the post commanding officer. Flanking it on either side were four duplex houses with a wide hall, capable of housing two families each when necessary.

Across the parade ground to the east were four U-shaped barracks for enlisted men, laid out to accommodate four companies—cavalry, infantry, or a combination of both. East of the barracks, separated by a lane, were quarters for the laundresses and married soldiers, administrative offices, bakery, prison, guardhouse, chapel, storehouses, and corrals with wooden stables for two hundred horses. Just south of this complex of buildings stood the six-ward, thirty-six-bed hospital, which served all the personnel at Fort Union. A staff of eight, including a surgeon and assistant surgeon, made this one of the best hospitals in the West.

Quartermaster Depot

The parade ground extended north into the Fort Union Quartermaster Depot, which supplied all the New Mexico forts. It boasted a much larger physical plant than the Fort Union post and employed considerably more men, mostly civilians.

In line with the post officers' quarters were the depot officers' quarters and commissary offices. The three duplex quarters housed officers of the supply depot and their families. Built on the same general plan as the commanding officers' quarters, each had four spacious rooms on each side of a wide central hall. The quartermaster, as commanding officer of the depot and in charge of all construction, had the finest residence at Fort Union. The three commissary office buildings, aligned with post and depot officers' quarters, continued the treatment of columned porticos.

Across the extended parade ground from the depot officers' quarters and commissary offices, in line with the post barracks, were four large storehouses and the mechanics' corral, which consisted of shops and quarters for blacksmiths, carpenters, and wheelwrights. A sundial on the parade grounds is centered on the quartermaster's quarters. Behind this group of buildings was the transportation corral, with sheds for freight wagons, storage houses for grain, and quarters for the teamsters. This was the service area for the thousands of draft animals required each year to supply the frontier army with goods from the East. Half of the original corral was destroyed by fire in 1874. The army subsequently tore down the other half and rebuilt the whole complex of adobe brick. The new corral met the diminished needs of the fort through the remainder of its life as a military post.

Ordnance Depot

By comparison with the Post and Quartermaster Depot, the Fort Union Arsenal in the Ordnance Reserve, which served the ordnance needs of the department, was a modest establishment. It consisted of an officer's house, a barracks building, storehouses, shops, and magazine, all surrounded by a 4,000-square-foot wall.

Fine as the elaborate new Fort Union appeared, it had been too hastily constructed. The main trouble lay in faulty roofing, which admitted water to the adobe walls and started an eroding action that made constant repairs necessary. Fort Union continued to grow for another twenty years and to serve as a tactical base and supply depot on the New Mexico frontier.

PECOS

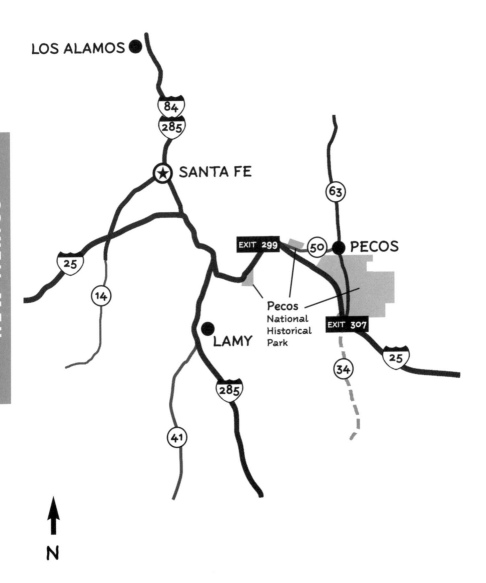

LOS ALAMOS

84
285

SANTA FE

25

14

63

EXIT 299   50   PECOS

Pecos
National
Historical
Park

LAMY

EXIT 307

285

34

25

41

N

NEW MEXICO

5

Pecos
National Historical Park

Pecos, San Miguel County, New Mexico
www.nps.gov/peco

Pecos National Historical Park is in north-central New Mexico, 25 miles southeast of Santa Fe, off I-25. When traveling north on I-25, take exit 299 on Highway 50, go five miles to the town of Pecos, turn south on Highway 63, and travel two miles to the park. When traveling south on I-25, take exit 307, and travel five miles north on Highway 63 to the park.

] "There is no known ruin which seems to have been lived in continuously for so long a period." [

Alfred Vincent Kidder, *An Introduction to the Study of Southwestern Archaeology: With a Preliminary Account of the Excavations at Pecos* (1924)

The massive ruins of a Franciscan mission established in the seventeenth century on a ridge in the Pecos River Valley, set against the Sangre de Cristo Mountains to the north and Glorietta Mesa to the south, is an arresting sight of towering adobe walls. But there is much more to see at this unusual national park system unit. Alongside the soaring mission walls built in the early 1700s are remnants of a sprawling *convento* and pueblo. These are the centerpieces of Pecos National Historical Park, overlaid with 12,000 years of southwestern history.

In more than 6,600 acres, the park's three units include the ruins of the Pecos Pueblo—the easternmost pueblo visited by Francisco Coronado in 1541—remnants of two missions, a six-mile stretch of the Santa Fe Trail, 1.5 miles of the Pecos River, Civil War sites at Apache Canyon and Glorietta Battlefield, an 1850s ranch that also served as a stage station, and a 1930s ranch house in Pueblo

Ruins at Pecos.

Revival style. The visitor center contains a fine museum with artifacts from the site. Pecos National Monument was designated in 1965 and, with the expansion of the original four hundred acres, declared a National Historical Park in 1990. Pecos Pueblo and Glorietta Pass Battlefield are National Historic Landmarks.

Visitor center.

SETTLEMENT AT PECOS

Sometime after A.D. 800, Puebloan settlers moved into the upper Pecos River Valley to form small, scattered pithouse settlements. The valley was a gateway to the Rio Grande Valley, a strategic location between the agricultural Pueblo communities of the northern Rio Grande and the nomadic hunting tribes of the plains. Serving as a trading and cultural center between the Rio Grande pueblos to the west and the Plains Indians to the east, the Pecos Indians prospered. Over the centuries, the population slowly grew. Around 1100, Anasazi settlers arrived and built pueblos of sandstone walls over the ruins of smaller villages.

By the time the Spanish conquistadors arrived in 1540, the ridge held two major pueblo structures that rose four and five stories, housing two thousand people. The larger multilevel north pueblo, surrounded by a defensive perimeter wall, contained nearly seven hundred rooms and several kivas built around central plazas. After Coronado departed to search for the fabled cities of Cibola, Pecos was spared further contact with Spaniards until 1590, when Castano de Sosa stormed and occupied the pueblo with a small, well-armed force. After nearly sixty years, the Spaniards had returned to convert the Indians and colonize their lands. In his account of the expedition, de Sosa wrote that the pueblo

Arched doorway in church wall.

was arranged in house blocks, four to five stories in height, each block with fifteen or sixteen rooms, which the inhabitants reached by ladders that could be drawn up after them.

Between 1617 and 1717, the Franciscans built four churches. The largest—south of the pueblo at Pecos—was finished in 1625 by Fray Andres Juarez. The Indians answered the conflicting demands of the Spanish to choose between the "cross and sword" with the Pueblo Revolt of 1680, when the Indians united to drive the Spaniards back into Mexico. The Spaniards returned twelve years later under Diego de Vargas and rebuilt a smaller church over the remains of the one destroyed in the uprising, the one seen standing today. From then to the end of Spanish rule, the majority of the Pecos Indians were partners with the Spaniards as allies and traders with surrounding tribes.

By the 1780s, disease, Comanche raids, and migration had reduced the Pecos population to fewer than three hundred. The settlement was almost a ghost town when the Santa Fe trade began flowing past it in 1821; the last survivors departed in 1838, leaving a decaying pueblo and an empty mission church. They joined their relatives at Jemez Pueblo, eighty miles west, where their descendents live today.

The expanded National Historical Park includes Kozlowski's Stage Station, a tavern and watering stop on the Santa Fe Trail. Two nearby units preserve sites of the Civil War action at Glorietta Pass in March 1862. There, Union forces turned back a Confederate invasion attempting to capture military supplies from Union forts in New Mexico and to recruit New Mexicans, Utah Mormons, and Colorado miners to the Confederate cause.

HISTORIC STRUCTURES

Knowledge of the long-disappeared pueblo and the standing remains of the massive, adobe walls of the fourth church on the site comes from contemporary comments of Spanish visitors, Santa Fe Trail travelers, the work of archeologist Alfred Vincent Kidder, and a recent technologically advanced examination of the site and excavation records. As recently as 1967, the footings of the 1622 church were uncovered around the foundations of today's mission ruins, confirming tales of the existence of a much larger church on the site.

Alfred Vincent Kidder

Alfred ◆ —— Vincent —— ◆ Kidder

Alfred Vincent Kidder is revered for his pioneering archeological work, a reputation founded on his excavations at Pecos Pueblo. He first began his work in the Southwest in 1907 while a student at Harvard, when southwestern archeology was changing from artifact collecting into a field of systematic research and analysis. Sponsored at first by the Peabody Museum of Harvard University, Kidder was appointed director of excavations at the Pecos ruins for the Phillips Academy at Andover, Massachusetts, in 1915, a position he held until 1929.

Kidder began to excavate at Pecos in 1915, and his workers spent the next twelve seasons at the site. Remains of the pueblo, trash mounds, and ruins of the last mission and convent offered the opportunity to test his theory of dating by stratigraphy on a large scale. Examining layer upon layer of pottery and other remains, Kidder dated the site and worked out the general time sequence of many other southwestern sites. In addition to his excavations, Kidder developed a multidisciplinary approach, including anthropologists and other scientists. To gain another perspective for analysis of the pueblo, he engaged Anne and Charles Lindbergh for aerial photography. Work at the excavation led Kidder to publish *An Introduction to the Study of Southwestern Archaeology: With a Preliminary Account of the Excavations at Pecos* (1924), now a classic in American archeology.

Kidder's work at Pecos is considered to have laid the foundation for modern archeological field methods. In 1927, he invited archeologists and ethnologists working on sites throughout the Southwest to the Pecos field camp to develop a classification system that helped identify cultural development of southwestern people. The "Pecos Classification" of eight prehistoric periods, Basketmaker I through III and Pueblo I through V, is still used today. The Pecos Conference, held annually, returns to Pecos every five years.

Pecos Pueblo

Today, a walk through the pueblo ruins reveals rough, poorly fitting stones in uneven rows, marking the lower tiers of the two-terraced community houses that once towered three to four stories high. Reconstructed from Spanish conquistador accounts by Pedro de Castañeda, chronicler of the Coronado expedition in 1541, the pueblo is described as follows:

> "It is square, perched on a rock, with a large court or yard in the middle, containing the *estufas* [kivas]. The houses are all alike, four stories high. One can walk on the roofs over the whole pueblo, there being no streets to prevent this. The second terrace is all surrounded with lanes which enable one to circle the whole pueblo. These lanes are like balconies which project out, and under which one can find shelter. The houses have no doors on the ground floor. The inhabitants use movable ladders to climb to the corridors, which are on the inner side of the pueblo. They enter them that way, as the doors of the houses open into the corridors on this terrace. The corridors are used as streets. The houses facing the open country are back to back with those on the patio, and in time of war they are entered through the interior ones. The pueblo is surrounded by a low wall of stone. There is a spring of water inside, which they are able to divert."

Kidder excavated a North and South Pueblo and several smaller adjacent room blocks. The North Pueblo is a large rectangular enclosure forming a quadrangle, and the South Pueblo is a long linear room block. These room blocks were approximately four stories high with 1,020 rooms, twenty-six kivas, and one enclosed plaza. Construction was of sandstone blocks from the mesa; pine and juniper logs from surrounding forests were used as columns and roof beams. Ground-floor rooms were used for storage or disposing trash; dwelling units were on upper floors. In one area, Kidder uncovered six levels of dwellings. He reported, "These people weren't builders, they were stackers. As one dwelling fell into ruins, a new one was simply constructed on top of the old one."

Mission Church and Convento

Now seen on the horizon as a reddish-tinted shape with its sloping buttresses emerging from the irregular profile of the adjacent *convento* ruins, Mission Nuestra Señora de Los Angeles de Porcíuncula dominates the top of the ridge at Pecos. It is the last of four mission churches on the ridge overlooking the Pecos River.

The standing church ruins have attracted and awed visitors for centuries. At its time of completion, the structure was the most imposing of New Mexico's mission churches and the largest in New Spain, with six bell towers and whitewashed buttressed walls rising fifty-five feet above the ridge. Travelers on the Santa Fe Trail passed the word back east about its soaring walls surrounded by pueblo remains. In his widely read *Explorations & Adventures in Arizona & New Mexico* about his southwest travels in the late 1850s, Samuel Woodsworth Cozzens perpetuated the Indian legend of a pueblo built by Montezuma: "Here stood the large Mexican temple, Montezuma's church, which was three stories high, and where burned the sacred flame day and night. The Indian legend is, that Montezuma built this pueblo himself, with his own hands."

Pecos church ruins in 1932.

In 1618, Franciscan monks established a mission just east of Pecos Pueblo and began building the first church, a small one that may never have been completed. Fray Juarez arrived in 1622 with grand plans for a "magnificent temple with six towers, three on each side." The church was 150 feet long from the entrance to the altar, with walls fifty-five feet high, and covered almost 6,000 square feet of space. This spacious structure was built with more than 300,000 adobe bricks in its eight- to ten-foot thick walls, supported by closely spaced buttresses that may have stood as high as forty-five feet. Alongside was the relatively small *convento*, with priests' quarters, workshops, a school, corrals, stables, a kitchen, kitchen garden, and dining room. The church was burned in the 1680 Indian rebellion, and a temporary chapel was built after the 1692 reconquest by the Spaniards.

The fourth church, the one seen today, was begun by Fray Jose de Arranegui in 1706 and completed in 1717. The rebuilt *convento* was twice the size of the earlier one, showing more emphasis on teaching trades to the Pecos people than on converting them. Long thought to be the fabled second church, it was not until 1967 that National Park Service archeologist Jean M. Pinkley uncovered foundations beneath the one standing wall. This church was much larger, and from indications of the foundations, was the only mission in New Mexico to have buttresses. This also matches a 1630 description of the Pecos church by Fray Alonso Benevides that, up to Pinkley's excavations, had been thought to be an exaggeration of the size of the church in order to impress the authorities in Mexico and Spain to obtain more money and help for the missions.

SALINAS PUEBLO MISSIONS

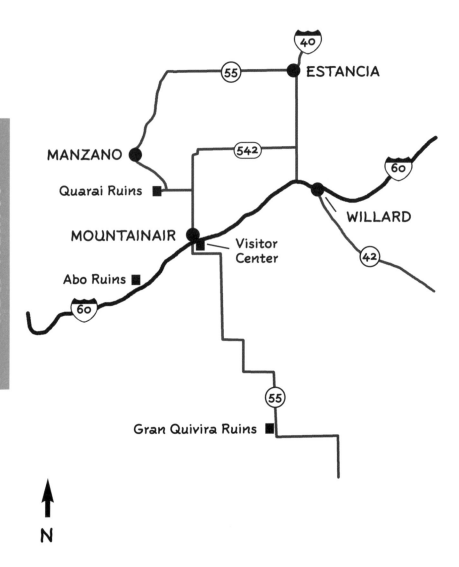

6

Salinas Pueblo Missions
National Monument

Mountainair, Torrance County, New Mexico
www.nps.gov/sapu

The Salinas Pueblo Missions National Monument Visitor Center at Mountainair can be reached by taking I-25 south from Albuquerque to Belen, then Highway 47 diagonally to U.S. 60, then east 21 miles to Mountainair. Information on the Quarai, Abó, and Gran Quivira ruins, as well as the surrounding area, is provided by National Park Service rangers at all three ruins and park headquarters. Abó ruins are 9 miles west on U.S. 60 and one-half mile north on Highway 513. Gran Quivira ruins are 26 miles south on Highway 55. Quarai ruins are 8 miles north on Highway 55 and 1 mile west.

"Of the various bits of evidence concerning the seventeenth-century friars, . . . the most eloquent are the isolated ruins of such missions as Abó, Las Humanas, and Pecos—massive monuments to the zeal of the friars, situated in the midst of a loneliness akin to what they knew."

Friar Hans Lentz, OFM, "Franciscan Missiology in Seventeenth-Century New Mexico," manuscript at Duns Scotus College, Southfield, Michigan, 1969

Salinas Pueblo Missions National Monument preserves the ruins of prehistoric Indian pueblos and three of the oldest, most intact seventeenth-century Spanish missions in the United States. Centered on park headquarters in Mountainair in north-central New Mexico, the present monument of 1,100 acres was established in 1980 through the combination of two New Mexico State Monuments (Abó and Quarai) and the former Gran Quivira National

SALINAS PUEBLO MISSIONS

NEW MEXICO

ESTANCIA
WILLARD
MOUNTAINAIR

60
42
41
55
542
55

Salinas Pueblo Missions
National Monument

MANZANO

47
60

BELEN
BERNARDO
25

← N

Monument. The mission church ruins at Abó and Quarai are National Historic Landmarks.

The similarities in the three missions are deceptive. Each setting is different, each place distinctive and memorable in the remaining outlines of church and pueblo as evidence of the struggle between seventeenth-century church and civil authority and dominance over the native people. Although the ruins are spread over a radius of twenty-five miles from the visitor center, they are worth exploring for their rich history of Spanish New Mexico.

The surviving portions of the three churches have changed very little since their original construction. At all three missions the University of New Mexico, the Museum of New Mexico, and the National Park Service have stabilized the ruins and carried out some reconstruction. Most of the material altered or added to by reconstruction is along the tops of the walls. Only in a few places do additions and alterations obscure or change the appearance of the surviving structures.

THE PUEBLOS AND THE SPANIARDS

Millions of years ago, the Salinas Valley was a shallow lake. Climate changes dried the lake, leaving behind layers of limestone and salt beds (*salinas*). The Anasazi and Mogollon cultures overlapped in the valley and evolved into Tiwa- and Tompiro-speaking Puebloans. By the tenth century, members of the Mogollon culture were living there. A century later, the Anasazi culture began to assimilate the Mogollon. Over the next several centuries, Abó, Gran Quivira, and Quarai became the sites of pueblos, and the area thrived as a major trade center between the Rio Grande Valley to the west and the Plains Indians to the east. During this period, aboveground jacal structures made of brush chinked with mud were gradually replaced by circular multilevel pueblos with wedge-shaped rooms around a kiva. Later, these early pueblos were replaced by rectangular structures.

Early in the seventeenth century, Spanish Franciscans found northern New Mexico ripe for conversion of the Salinas Pueblo. Three of the missions established at the time are now included in the Salinas Pueblo National Monument: La Nuestra Señora de la Purisma Concepción de Quarai (Quarai), San Gregorio de Abó (Abó), and San Buenaventura and San Isidro at Gran Quivira (Gran Quivira), or Pueblo de las Humanas, as it was called in the seventeenth century. The other missions were at Chilili, Taxique, and Tabira.

Abó was a thriving community when the Spaniards first visited the Salinas Valley in 1581. Franciscans began converting Abó residents in 1622, and by the late 1620s, the first church had been built. Later, a second church was built, with a sophisticated buttressing technique unusual in seventeenth-century New Mexico.

Las Humanas was a major regional trading center with the Plains Indians from beyond the mountains to the east. The multistoried pueblos contained more than three thousand rooms that changed in shape over the years from round to square. At Gran Quivira (Las Humanas), the church of San Isidro was constructed between 1629 and 1631. The *convento* of this original mission was situated in a remodeled and extended portion of the house block north of the church. The new church and *convento* of San Buenaventura were begun in 1672, but never completed.

Settled around 1300, the pueblo at Quarai was populated by four to six hundred Indians. The church with its massive four- to six-foot-thick walls and towers was begun in 1629 and completed around 1632.

Weakened by the stress between Spanish colonists and the church, Apache raids, severe drought, famine, and disease, the Salinas pueblos came to an end in the 1670s. By the time of the Pueblo Revolt in 1680, the Salinas villages were empty, their peoples dispersed among the pueblos of the middle Rio Grande Valley.

After the abandonment by the Spaniards and Puebloan people, Lt. James W. Albert visited the Abó ruins in 1846. His careful watercolor of the church recorded a number of important details of the structure before deterioration had occurred. Maj. James H. Carleton visited Abó on his way to Las Humanas in December 1853. His detailed description of the church again recorded information of great importance to a history of the buildings.

THE MISSIONS

The Salinas Valley mission churches built in the first half of the seventeenth century exist now only as ruins. All of the same character, with walls constructed of comparatively small thin stones, they are different in their architecture from any others built under Spanish influence in New Mexico.

The red stone walls of Abó church, supported by buttresses, form a 132-foot-long nave. Mission churches of San Isidro and San Buenaventura at the pueblo of Las Humanas (Gran Quivira) are the remains of an unaltered seventeenth-century Franciscan temporary church and a full-sized church and *convento*. The massive walls of Quarai, in red Abó stone, are intact enough to form an enclosure, offering you an experience of the nave as felt by the Pueblo Indians more than three centuries ago. The preserved condition of the ruins offers an excellent example of Franciscan architecture.

Ruins of the church at Abó.

Abó

Fray Francisco Fonte arrived in New Mexico in the autumn of 1621. Assigned to the pueblo of Abó, he negotiated with the authorities in the pueblo to build a mission complex. He arranged several rooms at the east end of the pueblo for his first *convento*, and the area just east as the site for the permanent church and *convento*. The people of Abó accepted his presence and some groups aided him in the construction of the new rooms of the temporary *convento*. In 1623, he began planning a permanent church and *convento* dedicated to San Gregorio.

Fonte worked out a simple plan for a rather small church and *convento*.

Spanish
◆ — Mission — ◆
Churches

Planning a mission involved negotiations with the Indians to build near pueblos. Once a location was settled on, the Franciscan friar laid out the mission's two parts: the church and the *convento*. The design and construction of the mission combined the Spanish architectural tradition of wall-and-beam construction with traditional local Indian building methods and materials.

Larger than other interior spaces experienced by the Pueblo Indians, churches were built to impress them with the new religion and the monotheistic nature of Christianity. By entering from the bright daylight into a long narrow hall, one's attention was focused on the sanctuary and altar opposite the main entrance doors. Churches varied in plan—simple parallelograms or cruciform with transepts. The main altar was usually raised above the level of the nave on a platform reached by broad stairs. To either side of the main altar, the Franciscans built secondary altars called collaterals, or side altars. At the front of the church over the entrance was usually a choir loft, reached by a stairway built under the loft or in a room against the outside wall of the church.

The transept and altar roof were a few feet higher than the roof over the nave, where the people stood, and accommodated a clerestory opening in the space between the two roof levels. This window, not visible to the congregation, focused a dramatic beam of light on the altar and the decorations around it. Church interiors were more colorful than the drab, adobe-tan exteriors. A layer of tan clay plaster coated the clay floor and stone walls, and the walls were painted with a thin white plaster coat.

An exception to typical mission construction of adobe bricks, the Salinas churches used available stone, explaining the state of preservation despite abandonment for more than three centuries. Exterior walls of core-and-masonry veneer construction, three to four feet thick at the foundations, supported roof construction of *vigas*, *latillas*, and a covering of grass, bundles of reeds, and dirt.

The main *convento*, built next to the church and often sharing common walls, included the Franciscan community residence, kitchen, dining room, storerooms, workshops, school, and infirmary. Adjacent to the main convento complex, a second courtyard contained food storage buildings, corrals, stables, and animal pens.

Because of the gentle slope of the site, he based his plan on a low artificial platform, somewhat like those later used at Quarai and Las Humanas. The church faced almost exactly south. It was 25 feet wide and 83.5 feet long on the interior, without transepts. Walls of core-and-veneer (small, flat-shaped stones) were an average thickness of about three feet along the sides of the nave and 2.8 feet along the front and apse ends of the church. The walls stood about twenty-five feet high to the undersides of the nave roof *vigas*, and twenty-eight feet to the tops of the parapets along the nave. The roof structure was supported on square beams resting on corbels, with a spacing of about two feet between *vigas*. A

The kiva in the convento at Abó.

clerestory window, about sixty feet from the front of the church, was inserted in the four-foot-high space between the nave roof and higher transept roof.

The apse at the north end of the nave measured 12 by 12 feet, tapering only slightly so that the width of the north end was 11 feet on the interior. Centered against its north side, a large buttress five feet across and almost three feet thick supported the forty-foot-high apse walls. A simple porch and choir balcony were built inside the front of the church. Outside the front of the church, Fonte added a *campo sancto* (cemetery), 110 by 100 feet, and a porch platform with stairs centered on the church, 77 feet wide and extending 18 feet south from the façade of the church. The *convento* east of the church underwent several reconstructions through 1672. Frequent room renovations and other additions created a sprawling

Restored red sandstone ruins of Mission San Gregorio de Abó.

complex of rooms around two courtyards.

About 1640, Fray Francisco Acevedo became guardian of Abó. He soon began planning a renovation of the San Gregorio church and *convento*. Acevedo designed the large impressive church he wanted by adding to the present church to minimize additional stonework. The additions included transept-like side chapels, a larger, more intricate group of altars, and a higher, more imposing roof for more space and light in the nave. He moved the baptismal font and the choir stairs to separate rooms outside the church, leaving more space under the choir loft. The additional width was sufficient to allow three full-sized altars: two collaterals and an imposing high altar in the center. The location of the main altar and the height of the walls of the church required the relocation of the clerestory in order for the sunlight to illuminate the area during the Christmas feast-days.

On an expedition to investigate the Salinas district in 1853, Maj. J. H. Carleton came upon Abó at dusk. "The tall ruins," he wrote, "standing there in solitude, had an aspect of sadness and gloom. The cold wind . . . appeared to roar and howl through the roofless pile like an angry demon." Carleton recognized the remains as a Christian church, but didn't know that the "long heaps of stone, with here and there portions of walls projecting above the surrounding rubbish," marked the remains of a large pueblo.

Gran Quivira

The rugged rocky ridge called Las Humanas by the Puebloans differs from the other red Abó stone Salinas missions with the distinctive uniformity of its blue-gray limestone walls. Gran Quivira (also known as Las Humanas), the largest of the Salinas pueblos, was an important trade center for many years before and after the Spanish *entrada*. Ancient southwestern Anasazi and Mogollon cultures had roots here as far back as seven thousand years. South and west of this ridge, archeologists found the remains of many pithouses dating from A.D. 700 or 800

The entrance of San Buenaventura mission church at Gran Quivira.

Convento walls and the never completed church at Gran Quivira.

to about 1300. The occupants of the pithouses were apparently from the Jornada branch of the Mogollon culture, whose primary settlements were farther south. The change to aboveground construction of multilevel pueblos began around 1300, with construction of masonry houses built with a yellow caliche mortar, first laid out in concentric circles and then later, beginning in the 1400s, in rectangles around courtyards and kivas. The population of the pueblo eventually reached 1,500 or more people.

According to historical records, two early Spanish expeditions reached Pueblo de Las Humanas. In 1598, Don Juan de Oñate accepted the village's allegiance to the Spanish king and probably collected tribute. In 1629, two years after Fray Alonso de Benevides introduced the new Christian religion to the Indians, Fray Francisco Letrado became the first resident priest at Las Humanas, converting eight remodeled rooms of a pueblo for the Franciscan's quarters. Letrado continued conversion efforts and "established there a *convento* and a fine church," according to records. This "fine church" was planned as a simple parallelogram, containing a nave and chapel. Attached to the east was the *convento*. Work was underway when Letrado left Las Humanas in 1631; he was martyred the next spring. Around 1636, Fray Francisco Acevedo of Abó completed this church dedicated to San Isidro. The pueblo could not support the mission and it lapsed into a *visita* (parish church).

At the end of July 1659, Fray Diego de Santandér arrived at Las Humanas with his wagonload of supplies to get the mission started. Santandér planned a massive and imposing church, with an ample *convento* for the largest of the Las Humanas villages, dedicated as San Buenaventura. He selected a location on the west end of the small mesa, which sloped steeply down to the west and south. The site required a platform with retaining walls almost eight feet high along the west side and part of the north side, and six feet high along the south. Construction was incomplete when the mission and pueblo were abandoned in the late 1670s.

Maj. Carleton described the ruins:

"We found the ruins of Gran Quivira to consist of the remains of a large church, with a monastery attached to it; a smaller church or chapel [San Isidro]; and the ruins of a town extending 900 feet in a direction east and west and 300 feet which is found in the vicinity.

"The church is 140 feet long, outside, with the walls nearly six feet in thickness. . . . Like the churches at Abó and Clara [Quarai] it is constructed in the form of a cross, . . . The total length inside [is] 128 feet, 8 inches. The width of the nave is 27 feet. . . . A gallery extended along the body of the church for the first 24 feet. Some of the beams which sustained it and the remains of two of the pillars that stood along under the end of it which was nearest to the altar, are still here; the beams in a tolerably good state of preservation, but the pillars very much decayed; they are of pine wood and are very elaborately carved.

"There is also what might be called an entablature supporting each side of the gallery and deeply embedded in the main wall of the church . . . ; it is carved very beautifully, indeed, and exhibits not only skill but exquisite taste in the construction of the figures. The beams are square and carved on three sides. . . . The stone of which the great church was

Gran Quivira.

Quarai mission church.

built was not hewn nor even roughly dressed, but the smoothest side of each piece was laid to the surface with great care. We saw no one piece in all the ruins over a foot in length. The walls of the church are now about thirty feet in height. It was estimated that originally the building was all of fifty feet in height."

Time for the pueblo and the church was running out by 1670, when drought reduced the food supply, and resentment against the Spanish rule and suppression of the native people's beliefs was growing stronger. On September 3, 1670, Apaches raided the pueblo and Acevedo's *visita* church of San Isidro "was profaned and laid waste." Statues and paintings on the altar were destroyed, and vestments torn to pieces. Soon after the raid, the Franciscans and those Indians friendly to them moved to other missions and settlements in the Rio Grande Valley. The buildings of Las Humanas were left to collapse slowly into mounds of rubble. The unroofed permanent church slowly filled with sand and dirt blown in by the wind, and the scaffolding rotted and fell apart. Eventually the roofs of the *convento* collapsed, room by room, and wall rubble began to add itself to the growing fill in the rooms and church. Within a century, Las Humanas looked much like it does today.

Quarai

The mission church at Quarai, the most intact of the churches, stands solitary on a hilltop, offering you an experience of walking into the nave of a Salinas Mission church and feeling the overpowering size and vast space created by the Franciscans to impress the Indians. Stop for a moment to absorb the original flagstone floor, red-stone walls of massive thickness reaching almost to their original height, remains of towers, and visible sockets for beams tracing the choir loft and roofline. Walk the length of the hundred-foot-long nave to the rear of the altar wall and turn back to look at the main entry doorway, choir window, and corner bell towers. The soaring walls of carefully laid thin stones absorb all sound.

Fray Juan Gutiérrez de la Chico arrived at Quarai in 1626 and selected a mound of ruins left near the northeast corner of the pueblo as the site of his church and *convento*. During the remainder of 1626, Gutiérrez designed the new church and *convento* of La Purísima Concepción de Quarai. Construction began in 1627. The church, with its nave 104 feet by 50 feet and 26 feet high at the roof, rose along with the *convento*. The church's height, complexity of construction, and extensive interior decoration took three years to reach completion. Still, at the end of the third year of construction, the crews had completed the *convento*, but the church stood only to a height of about 13 feet.

Quarai.

Eventually, façade towers reached a height of 39 feet, the nave towers 143 feet, and the apse towers 45 feet. Reinforcing tower buttresses ten feet square at principal corners supported the relatively thin four-foot-thick walls. *Vigas* spanning the nave and clerestory window were from 37 to 56 feet in length. Because of its height and complex structure, the church would require three more years of work to complete the masonry, roofing, interior woodwork, plastering, and decoration.

As a final touch, Gutiérrez added painted decorations on the white wall plaster. When complete, these consisted of dados along the walls of the church, sacristy, and the choir loft stairwell, and probably painted *retablo* designs behind the main altar, the two side altars, and the sacristy altar. The paintings were executed in red, black, gray, yellow, orange, and probably blue, white, and green. The *retablo* designs would serve until the new mission could afford to order carved and painted wooden *retablos* custom-made to fit into the spaces left behind the altars.

When Mexican settlers arrived at Quarai in the 1820s, they found the roofs of the old mission church and *convento* had survived relatively intact after 125 years of abandonment. The ruins we see today began with changes made by the settlers and the results of Apache raids at the mission site at the end of the decade. They represent a case study in deterioration of a historic structure. A fire set in one of the raids severely damaged the church. Collapsing beams carried away stonework in the apse. Burned-out lintels damaged the stonework above the doors and windows and on the inner face of the buttress towers, making the stone softer and much more susceptible to water damage. Soon the entire wall above the higher openings, undermined by this decay, began to fall in; tall V-shaped gaps formed in the walls, marking the locations where doors and windows had been. The gaps above the choir loft entrance door and the east nave window left the east nave wall unsupported. Within a century, it fell into the nave.

TEXAS

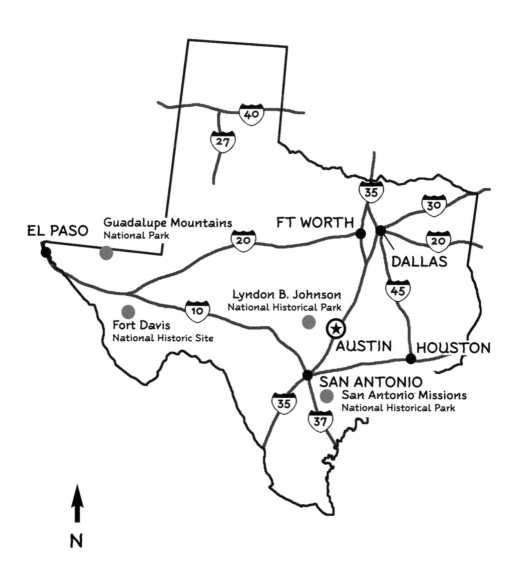

EL PASO

Guadalupe Mountains
National Park

FT WORTH

DALLAS

Lyndon B. Johnson
National Historical Park

Fort Davis
National Historic Site

AUSTIN

HOUSTON

SAN ANTONIO

San Antonio Missions
National Historical Park

N

FORT DAVIS

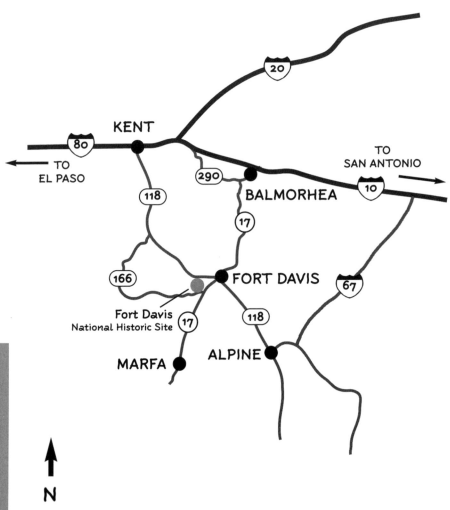

20

KENT

80

TO
EL PASO

TO
SAN ANTONIO

290

BALMORHEA

10

118

17

166

FORT DAVIS

67

Fort Davis
National Historic Site

17

118

MARFA

ALPINE

N

1

Fort Davis
National Historic Site

**In the western part of the state, in Fort Davis,
Jeff Davis County, Texas
www.nps.gov/foda**

Located on the north edge of the town of Fort Davis, the site can be reached via I-10 at the intersection of Texas Highways 118 and 17. From El Paso (about 4 hours), exit I-10 at Kent and take Texas 118 south. From San Antonio (about 7 hours), exit I-10 West to Balmorhea, then take Texas 17 and follow it to the fort.

] "Fort Davis had outlived its usefulness. And yet it is to be regretted that it was discontinued, owing to its salubrious climate." [

Brig. Gen. David S. Stanley, 1891

Fort Davis National Historic Site in west Texas is a long drive west from San Antonio or east from El Paso. Set in the rugged beauty of the Davis Mountains and rising from the flat sun-parched landscape at the foot of Sleeping Lion Mountain and the two-hundred-foot-high rock walls of Limpia Canyon, Fort Davis is considered one of the best remaining examples of a frontier military post in the American Southwest.

From 1854 to 1891, except for the Civil War years, Fort Davis guarded the Trans-Pecos segment of the southern route to California. The fort's strategic location on the San Antonio–El Paso Road protected immigrants, mail coaches, and freight wagons from raids by Mescalero Apaches and Comanches. Troops stationed at Fort Davis, including all-black regiments established after the Civil War—the Buffalo Soldiers—played a major role in the campaigns against Apache leader Victorio, with the Indian Wars in Texas coming to an end within a year after his death in October 1880.

Fort Davis in 1885.

More than sixty stone and adobe buildings were built on the plain at the foot of the mountains. In 1891, the fort was abandoned and the 447-acre Fort Davis National Historic Site containing the majority of the buildings, ruins, and foundations was authorized as a unit of the National Park System in 1961. Today, some twenty-five restored buildings of this National Historic Landmark, with twice as many foundations and ruins, are part of Fort Davis National Historic Site. Five of the restored buildings have been refurbished to appear much as they did in the 1880s.

FORT HISTORY

Following the Mexican-American War, claims to the vast region extending across modern-day Texas, New Mexico, Arizona, and California began to attract a trickle of immigrants that changed into a flood of travelers to the California gold fields. Avoiding the mountainous routes to the north, the San Antonio–El Paso Road was relatively flat and promised all-weather access as well as the wood and water of the Davis Mountains. Prompted by the hostile Apaches and Comanches, the War Department sent Bvt. Maj. Gen. Persifor Smith to west Texas to open a

TEXAS

184

Fort Davis parade ground in 1885.

series of posts. He selected Limpia Canyon for location of a post, establishing the presence of military forces in west Texas for the next five decades.

The first Fort Davis, established by the U.S. Army in 1854, was named in honor of the Secretary of War, Jefferson Davis. The post, garrisoned by Lt. Col. Washington Seawell and six companies of the 8th U.S. Infantry, was located in a box canyon near Limpia Creek on the eastern side of the Davis Mountains, where wood, water, and grass were plentiful. The location was tactically poor; Seawell preferred a location near a bubbling spring on the prairie opposite the mouth of the canyon, where eventually today's fort was built. With winter rapidly approaching, the building of the new post began in haste. The troops established a pinery in the mountains where trees were cut. The logs were then hauled by wagon to the fort. The first structures built were temporary shelters of oak and cottonwood pickets with grass-thatched roofs. All had packed-earth floors, while some had the luxury of glazed windows.

By 1856, six stone barracks with thatched roofs and flagstone floors had been erected in line immediately to the east of the parade ground. Foundations of several buildings from the first Fort Davis (1854–62) can be seen behind Officers' Row and west of the Post Hospital.

From 1854 to 1861, troops of the 8th Infantry spent much of their time in the field pursuing Comanches, Kiowas, and Apaches who terrorized travelers and attacked mail stations. In October 1855, Second Lt. Zenas R. Bliss, 8th U.S. Infantry, arrived at Fort Davis seventeen days after boarding the westbound stage in San Antonio. "The Post was the most beautifully situated of any that I have ever seen. It was in a narrow canyon with perpendicular sides, the walls of which were about 200 feet in height," the young officer later wrote. According to Lt. Bliss, life at Fort Davis in 1855 was exceedingly dull. The post was home to six companies of the 8th Infantry, the regimental band, and a number of officers, but only three officers' wives. "There were no parties or entertainments of any kind," Bliss wrote, and "not a house within one hundred miles" of the post. The young lieutenant remarked that although hunting in the area was good, "the Indians were so bad that no one ever thought of going more than three or four miles from the Post."

In attempting to adequately supply Fort Davis and other southwestern posts, the army embarked on an unusual experiment in 1855 involving the importation of camels from the Middle East. Under the command of Lt. Edward F. Beale, and with Fort Davis serving as a base of operations, the area west of San Antonio into New Mexico and Arizona was surveyed. The camels proved to be superior "beasts of burden," as they were able to carry heavier loads than horses, mules, or oxen, and they required less water and food. However, the "camel experiments," which were championed by Jefferson Davis, were short-lived. Although successful, they were ultimately forgotten with the onset of the Civil War.

At the outbreak of the Civil War in 1861 and Texas's secession from the Union, Confederate troops occupied the fort, serving at the post for a little more than a year while it functioned as a crucial supply depot for Gen. Henry H. Sibley's New Mexico campaign. In August 1862, Union forces regained control of the post when the Confederates failed to take New Mexico, but they did not occupy it. The deserted stone and pine huts were left vacant and vandalized for the next five years.

When Lt. Col. Wesley Merritt and four companies of the recently organized 9th U.S. Cavalry reestablished Fort Davis in June 1867, they chose a new location on the prairie at the mouth of Limpia Canyon. This is the site of the second and present fort and where Lt. Col. Seawell wanted the first fort to be constructed. About two hundred civilian carpenters, masons, and laborers started work on stone and adobe structures, and by March 1869, they had finished half of an ambitious plan when the department quartermaster ordered all work halted, probably for economic reasons. Not until the mid-1880s were all the buildings in place with construction of the hospital steward's quarters in 1877.

◆——The Camel Corps at Fort Davis ——◆

The naval officer who was in charge of the U.S. Camel Corps has become part of Fort Davis history. The suggestion of solving the problem of supply and transportation on the western desert with the use of camels saw daylight in the 1830s. In 1855, U.S. Secretary of War Jefferson Davis proposed a military camel corps, and Congress appropriated $30,000 to "purchase and import camels and dromedaries for the military" and to conduct experiments. In 1856, the first purchase of thirty-three camels from Tunis arrived at Indianola, Texas. A second drove of forty-four animals arrived the following year. Secretary of War John B. Floyd, the successor to Davis, ordered a wagon route surveyed from Fort Defiance, New Mexico, across the thirty-fifth parallel to the Colorado River, with collateral orders to test the dromedaries as pack animals at the same time. Command of the camels was transferred to a retired U.S. Navy lieutenant, Edward Fitzgerald Beale, who had served for several years as Superintendent of Indian Affairs in California. It was he who brought the first California gold east, and he had also explored Death Valley with Kit Carson. Thus, to Lt. Beale fell the honor of being the first and last commander of the U.S. Camel Corps.

Starting from a permanent camp and base of operations at Campe Verde, north of San Antonio, Beale took twenty-five camels as pack animals during an 1857 expedition, then on another in 1858 through 1859. Beale was enthusiastic about the camel's efficiency and endurance during these missions and later reconnaissance across the desert. The acting department commander, Bvt. Col. Robert E. Lee, wrote in 1860 that but for their "endurance, docility, and sagacity the reconnaissance would have failed."

The outbreak of the Civil War ended Jefferson Davis's camel experiment. Although nearly everyone, including horses and mules, hated the cantankerous camels, the test was actually successful. Camels could carry more and endure more hardship than any other beasts of burden, but their destiny was to fade away.

By 1890, there were more than sixty buildings at Fort Davis, with quarters for six companies of infantry and cavalry soldiers. Along one side of the post's five-hundred-foot-wide parade grounds was an officer's row of thirteen houses facing four enlisted men's barracks. Both rows of buildings were attractively embellished with columned porches facing the parade ground. The post hospital was built to the west of Officer's Row, farther into the mouth of the canyon. Other structures west of the San Antonio El Paso Road included the post trader's complex and telegraph office, post headquarters, chapel, bakery, and commissary. Quartermaster Storehouses, stables, and corrals were on the other side of the San Antonio–El Paso Road. Installation of an ice plant, gas street lamps, and a water system added a touch of civilization to the remote post.

Visitors to the fort today have the opportunity to tour restored and furnished buildings and view the foundation outlines of the first fort. The neatly aligned stone structures with white-trimmed columned and railed porches reflect the restoration and stabilization program of the National Park Service that began in 1963. The visitor center is located in what was originally an enlisted men's barracks. A restored barracks houses cavalry, infantry, artillery, transportation exhibits, and a furnished squad room and orderly room as it appeared in the summer of 1884 when occupied by Buffalo Soldiers of Troop H, 10th Cavalry.

Along Officer's Row, open for viewing are two restored and refurnished officer's quarters and behind Officer's Quarters #12 an officer's kitchen and storehouse has been restored and refurnished. The thirteen quarters facing the parade ground are fifty feet wide and twenty feet deep, some with rear extensions, kitchens, and privies in place. The main structures are uniformly built on tooled stone foundations, with volcanic tuff (Quarters 1, 2, 3, 5, 6, 7, and 8) or adobe walls (Quarters 4, 9, 10, 11, 12, and 13) and fireplaces at each end and wood-frame, shingled hip roofs. Tall window openings of double-hung multi-light sashes provided air circulation through the dwellings.

The Commanding Officer's Quarters, constructed by 1869, served as the residence for post commanders until 1891. The building is furnished to the period of 1882 to 1885, when Col. Benjamin H. Grierson, 10th Cavalry, served as post commander. A shared Lieutenants' Quarters was built for a captain in May 1882, but because of a shortage of housing, it was soon designated as a shared quarters. It is refurbished as if a bachelor lieutenant was living on the north side and a married lieutenant occupied the south half. Adjacent to Officer's Quarters No. 12 is a refurbished two-room Officer's Kitchen and Servant's Quarters. The building was separate from the main house because of cooking odors and the danger of fire.

The Commissary, located on the San Antonio–El Paso Road, contained food supplies for the garrison. While enlisted men received rations, officers and civilian employees could purchase food products at cost plus transportation. The commissary sergeant's office and the issue room are refurbished. The office occupied by the Acting Commissary of Subsistence (the officer in charge of the commissary office) contains interpretive exhibits.

Construction on the Post Hospital began in the mid-1870s. The twelve-bed north ward and central administrative ward was completed in 1876. A twelve-bed south ward was added in summer 1884. Constructed of adobe on a stone foundation, the hospital was located behind and west of Officers' Row. It had a tin roof, wooden flooring, and glass windows with curtains. Wide-columned porches gave it an airy spacious appearance. The hospital, normally staffed by a post surgeon, hospital steward, soldier-nurses, a cook or cooks, and a matron, represented state-of-the-art medicine of the nineteenth century.

"OUTLIVED ITS USEFULNESS"

Fort Davis's primary role of safeguarding the west Texas frontier against the Comanches and Apaches continued until 1881. Although the Comanches were defeated in the mid-1870s, the Apaches continued to make travel on the San Antonio–El Paso Road dangerous. Soldiers from the post regularly patrolled the road and provided protection for wagon trains and mail coaches. The last major military campaign involving troops from Fort Davis occurred in 1880. In a series of engagements, units from Fort Davis and other posts, under the command of Col. Benjamin Grierson, forced the Apaches and their leader Victorio into Mexico. There, Victorio and most of his followers were killed by Mexican soldiers.

With the end of the Indian Wars in west Texas, garrison life at Fort Davis became more routine. Soldiers occasionally escorted railroad survey parties, repaired roads and telegraph lines, and pursued bandits. In 1885, soldiers of the 10th Cavalry stationed at Fort Davis were ordered to Arizona to campaign against Geronimo. In June 1891, as a result of the army's efforts to consolidate its frontier garrisons, the post that had been occupied by the army for more than thirty years was ordered abandoned, having "outlived its usefulness."

After the fort was abandoned by the military, a series of caretakers took on the task of overseeing the old post. During the 1890s and early 1900s, many of the fort's buildings were occupied. The Post Hospital became a favorite spot for parties, picnics, and dances. The Post Chapel was used for Sunday and weeknight church services. By the mid-teens, however, many of the structures had fallen into disrepair. Plans to use the fort as a western movie set floundered during the depression. In 1953, the property was leased to the newly established Fort Davis

Officers' Row at Fort Davis today.

Historical Society. This organization had one major goal—the preservation of the old army post. For the next seven years, the society worked diligently to achieve this goal. Their efforts were rewarded in 1961 with the authorization of Fort Davis National Historic Site and establishment of the Site in 1963.

Never truly abandoned, the fort was spared the fate of other western army posts. Although photos from the 1950s show a huddle of derelict buildings, roofless and in disrepair, occupancy kept some roofs intact and stone construction preserved some buildings. In 1963, National Park Service preservation and stabilization work began on the buildings, with a decision to reconstruct missing portions of adobe buildings that were at least seventy percent intact. Porches were reconstructed, interiors restored, and adobe walls protected.

The reward for visitors to the pristine mountain landscape of Fort Davis National Historic Site is the sight of neatly aligned buildings facing the parade grounds and a flag snapping smartly in the prairie wind as it did 125 years ago. During the summer, park rangers and volunteers dressed in period-type clothing provide living-history demonstrations. It is a worthwhile trip to see one of the most extensive and impressive of any western frontier posts.

GUADALUPE MOUNTAINS

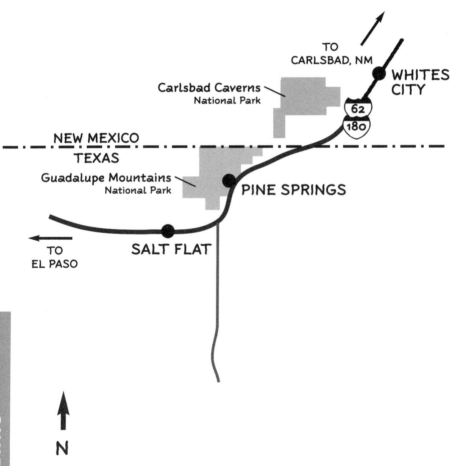

TO
CARLSBAD, NM

WHITES
CITY

Carlsbad Caverns
National Park

62
180

NEW MEXICO
TEXAS

Guadalupe Mountains
National Park

PINE SPRINGS

SALT FLAT

TO
EL PASO

N

2

Guadalupe Mountains
National Park

The park is located in west Texas on the Texas–New Mexico state line, near Pine Springs, Culberson County, Texas.
www.nps.gov/gumo

The Park Visitor Center at Pine Springs is located on U.S. 62 and 180, 110 miles east of El Paso and 55 miles southwest of Carlsbad, New Mexico.

"The most beautiful spot in Texas."

Attributed to a realtor describing the Guadalupe Mountains to Wallace E. Pratt

THE PARK

Texans treasure the Guadalupe Mountains as a well-kept secret, admiring its distinctive majesty towering into the west Texas sky above the Chihuahuan Desert. The National Park Service hails the mountains as a place where "a visitor can delight in grand views, diverse landscapes, and small pleasures." Texas geologist Wallace E. Pratt enjoyed the scenic beauty and wanted to share it with the entire country, donating over five thousand acres and promoting the idea of a park until its establishment in 1972.

Today, the 86,416-acre park is a rewarding journey to west Texas to experience the contrasting desert and the mountain range's stunningly beautiful canyons and lushly forested highlands. Like the prow of a great ship rising from the desert floor, El Capitan's steep cliffs are a traveler's landmark. In 1858, a traveler seeing El Capitan for the first time wrote: "It seemed as if

GUADALUPE MOUNTAINS

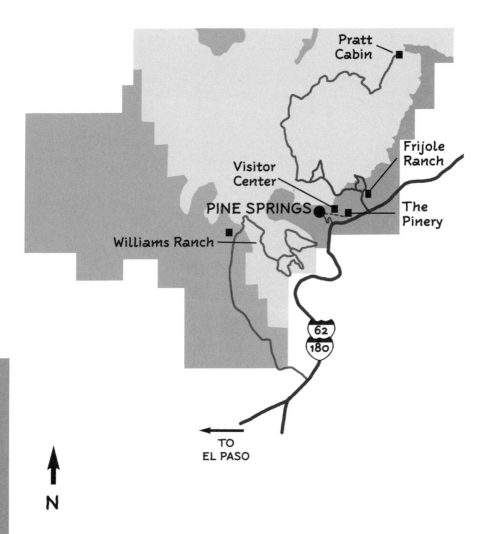

Pratt Cabin

Frijole Ranch

Visitor Center

PINE SPRINGS

The Pinery

Williams Ranch

62
180

TO EL PASO

N

TEXAS

nature had saved all her ruggedness to pile up in this colossal form. . . ."

The highest and southernmost portion of the V-shaped Guadalupe Mountains, a range that extends northeasterly into New Mexico, includes Guadalupe Peak, the highest point in Texas (8,749 feet), and other sheer cliffs and peaks more than 8,000 feet high. McKittrick Canyon and other escarpments and canyons of the high country, the relict forest in the Bowl, a rich diversity of flora and fauna, wilderness area (fifty-five percent of the park), and a collection of historic structures provide a rewarding journey's end. Guadalupe Mountains National Park contains portions of the world's most extensive and significant Permian limestone fossil reef, which also shaped Carlsbad Caverns, only forty miles to the north. At one point, the boundaries of the two parks are only five miles apart.

PARK HISTORY

For centuries, the remote Guadalupe Mountains were the exclusive domain of the Mescalero Apaches (the Nde). This changed in the mid-1880s when westward-bound immigrants came into contact with the Nde. The mountain's water and shelter were a staging ground for attacks against the pioneers, and a thirty-year campaign by the U.S. Army ended in 1880 with the last of the Nde driven out of the Guadalupes.

During this conflict, the Butterfield Overland Mail Line began service between St. Louis and San Francisco. The ruins of the Guadalupe Butterfield Stage Station, the "Pinery," in service from 1858–59, are near the visitor center. Ranching came to the Guadalupes after the Civil War and the Indian Wars. Only a short distance from the visitor center, accessible by vehicle from U.S. 62/180, the 1870s Frijole Ranch complex serves as a cultural history center, preserving artifacts of frontier life. A seven-mile four-wheel drive to the mountain's western escarpment leads to the remote historic Williams Ranch. Along the McKittrick Canyon Trail, approximately seven miles north of the visitor center off U.S. 62/180 and two and three-quarter miles from the trailhead, is the stone cabin built by geologist Walter E. Pratt. Along the road to the trail is the "Arm Waving Spot," where Pratt's employees noticed that the place "just naturally seemed to make geologists want to wave their arms around."

◆——— An Inland Reef ———◆

The Guadalupe Range is part of an ancient fossil bed, dating to the Permian Period about 250 million years ago. The four-hundred-mile-long, horseshoe-shaped Capitan Reef is a natural phenomenon formed from marine fossils deposited over millions of years in the Permian Sea covering portions of Texas and Mexico. Unlike modern barrier reefs of South Sea atolls derived mostly from a rigid framework of coral, the precipitated limestone of Capitan Reef was largely formed from skeletons of tiny organisms.

Eventually, the sea evaporated, leaving the reef covered under a thick

Guadalupe Canyon.

layer of sediments of mineral salts gypsum beds and petroleum buried deep below the surface. Another process underway during the reef's formation was the seeping of acidic water into cracks in the limestone, lacing the Guadalupe Mountains with caves, including Carlsbad Caverns to the north of Guadalupe Mountains National Park. About 26 million years ago, uplift moved the Capitan Reef nearly two miles from its original position, exposing it to wind and rain and eroding softer sediments until the resistant limestone reef was uncovered. The uplift faults are nearly vertical and range from two thousand feet to a mile or more, which today tower over the desert floor.

Visited by geologists from all over the world, it is considered one of the finest examples of an ancient marine fossil reef on Earth. The rock exposures excite "arm-waving" geologists with revelations of changes in rock types in Permian Period strata.

Williams Ranch, an anomaly on the West Texas landscape.

HISTORIC STRUCTURES
Frijole Ranch History Museum

The Frijole Ranch complex preseerved as a museum offers a view of frontier life in remote west Texas. A house, outbuildings, and a school were the center of life for the area's ranchers and farmers. The complex is at the end of a mile-long unpaved road off U.S. 62 and 180, about two miles north of the visitor center.

In 1876, near Frijole Spring, the bachelor Rader brothers built the front portion of the present ranch house using local stone. The Raders were the earliest cattle ranchers in this area of the southern Guadalupes. A succession of owners changed and added to the original stone structure. Around 1925, the Smith family took over the ranch and added some new outbuildings—a bunkhouse, double toilet, pumphouse, and wall—all built of rubble stone masonry. During the same time period, the Smiths also constructed a frame springhouse and schoolhouse. While the Smiths lived at Frijole, their home served as a community center and also as the local post office. At the time that the federal government acquired the property, Frijole Ranch was the headquarters for J. C. Hunter Jr.'s Guadalupe Mountains Ranch.

The Raders' house consisted only of the present front, or south-facing, living and dining rooms of the structure. It had double walls of native stone with a filler of mud between; interior walls were also plastered with mud. In 1906, John Thomas Smith and his family moved onto the property and made a living by truck farming, with a fifteen-acre orchard and garden east and north of the house. Periodically, the Smiths would load up their wagons in the evening, covering fresh produce with wet paper and linen, and travel sixty-five miles south, a two-day trip, to Van Horn to market.

The Smith family greatly expanded the Frijole Ranch House in the 1920s, adding a rear kitchen, two bedrooms, a second story, and dormers. A gable roof with wood shakes eventually covered the house. Outbuildings were added to the ranch, all constructed of stone masonry with shed roofs, including the luxurious double privy. The red schoolhouse was built with vertical wood siding and a low-pitched roof covered with corrugated tin. Up to eight children from the Smith family and local ranches once attended school there. Later, the schoolhouse served as a storage shed and bunkhouse. Although not built until 1950, the present barn complements the other buildings and is of wood-frame construction. A stone masonry wall encloses most of the Frijole Ranch complex.

In 1942, after thirty-six years, John Smith sold the Frijole Ranch house and associated property to Judge Jesse Coleman Hunter, who had begun buying land in the Guadalupe Mountains in 1923; by the 1940s, he owned 43,000 acres, including the Frijole Ranch. His "Guadalupe Mountains Ranch" concentrated on raising Angora goats, sheep, cattle, and horses. In 1945, J. C. Hunter's son, J. C. Hunter Jr., inherited the ranch and took an active interest in his lands in the Guadalupe Mountains. By 1965, he had purchased additional lands, and the Guadalupe Mountain Ranch totaled 67,312 acres. In 1966, he sold the ranch to the National Park Service for $1.5 million, about $22 per acre.

From 1969 to 1980, the ranch house served as a ranger residence. During the next three years, the National Park Service completed rehabilitation and renovation of the Frijole Ranch. Park staff used the ranch house as an operations office from 1983 until 1991. The Frijole Ranch House was again renovated in 1992, finally opening to the public as a history museum.

Butterfield Stage Station Ruins—"The Pinery"

At the 5,534-foot Guadalupe Pass, the Pinery was the highest station on the original 2,795-mile Butterfield route. Named for nearby stands of pine, the abundant Pine Spring water and good grazing made it one of the most favorably situated stations on the route from St. Louis to San Francisco. Although the ruins of the walls, about a half-mile walk from the visitor center, are all that is left of the 1858 Butterfield Overland Mail Stage Station, the place evokes the short life of the station at the foot of the Guadalupe Mountains. The Butterfield Mail Coach continued to come through the Pinery for eleven months until August 1859, when this route was abandoned for a new road that passed by way of Forts Stockton and Davis, which were better protected against Indian attacks. But long after its abandonment, the old Pinery Station continued to be a retreat for immigrants, freighters, soldiers, outlaws, renegades, and drovers.

The fortress-like Pinery Station, built of local limestone slabs and adobe walls, formed a rectangular enclosure with a single entrance. The three mud-roofed rooms were attached, lean-to fashion, to the inside walls, thirty inches thick and eleven feet high, which afforded safety and protection from Indian raids. The station's water supply came from Pine Spring through an open ditch to a tank inside the station. A stockade of heavy pine posts protected the main entrance on the south. In the southeast corner of the enclosure, a thatched shelter covered the wagon repair shop and smithy.

Stand among the ruins and imagine that afternoon on September 28, 1858, when the conductor of the first westbound Butterfield Overland Mail Coach sounded his bugle to announce the coach's arrival at the Pinery. Riding under Butterfield's command to his drivers—"Remember, boys, nothing on God's earth must stop the mail!"—they had traveled either fifty-six miles from the west or twenty-six miles from the east. Station masters and their crews were elated by the relief from isolation, travelers could take relief from the jolting ride with a warm meal, and the weary horses could be exchanged for fresh stock.

Imagine the feeling of isolation experienced by the stationmasters and their crews, and the sense of excitement and companionship brought by the stages. Between Fort Chadborne and El Paso, a distance of 458 miles, there was no sign of habitation other than outpost stage stations. The stage route between Fort Smith, Arkansas, and San Francisco, California, passed through only two real towns: Tucson and El Paso. One stretch of route had no settlements for nine hundred miles; another had no water for seventy-five.

The ruins are now a fragile remnant of a period of time before transcontinental telegraph and railroad lines spanned the country, a race to cross the continent with passengers and mail as stagecoaches challenged a hostile route and Pony Express riders romantically dashed across the West.

Williams Ranch

The Williams Ranch on the western side of the Guadalupes, standing among the rugged foothills five thousand feet below Guadalupe Peak, captures the isolation of west Texas ranching operations. The eight-mile-long drive from the visitor center offers excellent views of the Chihuahuan Desert landscape, and ends with the stark historic presence of a lonely and isolated ranch house. During most of the year the road is suitable only for four-wheel-drive vehicles; the remainder of the time a high-clearance pickup truck is required. You have to borrow a key at the visitor center to the entrance gates to visit the house.

Approaching the house, well preserved by the dry desert air, a common reaction among visitors is that the steeply gabled structure looks out of place in west Texas. Possibly, the builder was recalling wood-frame houses back east when he hauled lumber by mule train from Van Horn, Texas. Records are scarce but it is believed that John Smith of El Paso may have built the ranch house in 1908 for Henry Belcher and his wife, Rena. The family moved in with a wood stove, bunk beds, and other furniture, as well as wallpaper, a luxury for the time. The Belchers remained for about a decade and maintained a substantial ranching operation, at times supporting up to three thousand head of longhorn cattle on the mountain slopes.

Ownership changed in 1915 and James Adolphus Williams (known to friends as "Uncle Dolph"), a lone cowman from Louisiana, acquired the house and ranch property. With his partner and friend, an Indian named Geronimo (not the legendary Apache leader), Williams raised cattle, sheep, and goats, and farmed a limited amount of land until his death in 1942. Judge J. C. Hunter then purchased the ranch, adding to his extensive holdings in the Guadalupe Mountains. In 1966, Judge Hunter's son sold the ranch to the National Park Service, who replaced the roof of the ranch house, stabilized its foundation, and regularly treats the exterior surfaces with wood preservative.

Pratt Cabin

Wallace E. Pratt, the first geologist hired by Humble Oil Company (now part of Exxon), came to McKittrick Canyon in 1921. Accompanied by a real estate agent who claimed the canyon was "the most beautiful spot in Texas," Pratt was attracted by the beauty of the place and the geological history exposed in the canyon walls. Purchasing the land with partners, he planned a vacation home, eventually built in 1931–32 on the floodplain at the junction of North and South McKittrick Canyons.

The "stone cabin," as Pratt called it, was designed by Houston architect Joseph Staub. It is made of only stone and wood. Heart-pine rafters, collar

Wallace Pratt's stone cabin in McKittrick Canyon.

beams, and sheathing to support the stone roof were shipped in from East Texas. The stone used in building the house was quarried outside the canyon at the base of the Guadalupe Mountains. Using his geologist's skills, Pratt selected "silty limestone, thin-bedded and closely jointed by clean vertical fractures." Workers scraped off the thin layer of earth to reveal the proper stones, then levered the blocks apart with crowbars. The joints made the blocks fit well, and Pratt noted that few required the stonemason's hammer or chisel. Once complete, the Pratts furnished the cabin with rough-plank reclining chairs, four beds, assorted hammocks, and a special table to seat twelve. Outdoors was a picnic table made of stone. Two other structures complete the cabin complex: a building that contains a two-car garage and caretaker's quarters, and a pumphouse. Stone fences border the property on the south and west.

Pratt planned to use the cabin as a retirement home, but a flood that trapped the family in the canyon for several days caused him to rethink his plans. In 1945, the "Ship of the Desert," a modern steel and stone house, was built outside the canyon. Pratt donated his lands to the National Park Service and, until his death in 1981, participated in the movement to establish a national park in the Guadalupe Mountains, separate from Carlsbad Caverns.

LYNDON B. JOHNSON

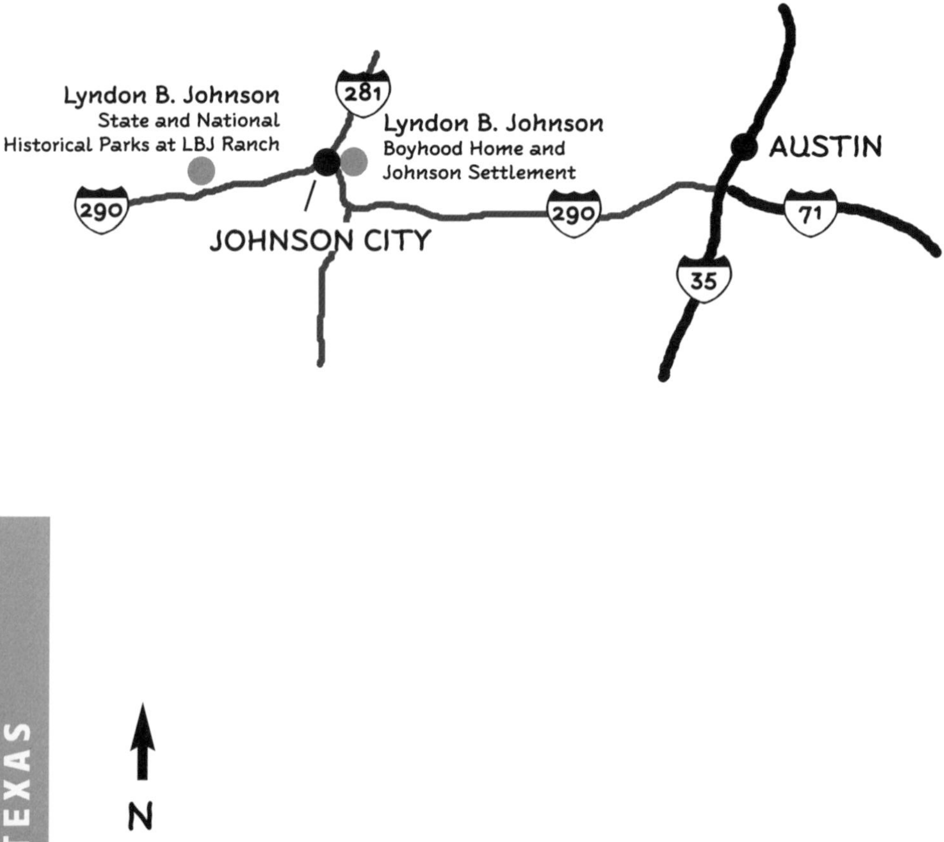

Lyndon B. Johnson
State and National
Historical Parks at LBJ Ranch

Lyndon B. Johnson
Boyhood Home and
Johnson Settlement

AUSTIN

290

281

290

71

JOHNSON CITY

35

TEXAS

↑
N

3

Lyndon B. Johnson
National Historical Park

The park is located in the Texas Hill Country in Johnson City Blanco County and Stonewall, Gillespie County, Texas.
www.nps.gov/lyjo

The Lyndon B. Johnson National Historical Park has two visitor areas separated by about 14 miles: the Johnson City District and the LBJ Ranch near Stonewall. The park visitor center in Johnson City is 50 miles west of Austin and 60 miles north of San Antonio. Tickets for the LBJ Ranch bus tour are purchased at the Lyndon B. Johnson State Park and Historical Site Visitor Center.

"It was once a barren land. The angular hills were covered with scrub cedar and a few live oaks. Little would grow in the harsh caliche soil. And each spring the Pedernales River would flood the valley. But men came and worked and endured and built."

Lyndon Baines Johnson,
36th President of the United States

The hilly area west of Austin, Texas—the Hill Country—had great meaning to Lyndon Baines Johnson. Here, the thirty-sixth president of the United States developed many of the traits of the southerner/westerner that history recorded in a great time of national stress. The approximately 1,570 acres, designated a national historical park in 1980, traces Johnson's family roots in the Hill Country where he spent his childhood; and is buried, his reconstructed birthplace; the Texas White House; and the ranching operations that continue today. The park offers a unique perspective into the complete life of an American president.

Lyndon B. Johnson National Historical Park has two sections: the LBJ Boyhood Home and the Johnson Settlement complex in the Johnson City Unit; and the LBJ Ranch Unit along the Pedernales River. You may want to trace the president's life chronologically, beginning with the Johnson Settlement and finishing the visit at the LBJ Ranch.

In Johnson City, from the LBJ Boyhood Home where Johnson lived from ages five to nineteen, you can walk to the Johnson Settlement, the LBJ's grandparents residence from 1865 to 1872. The Settlement's complex of restored historic structures traces the evolution of the Texas Hill Country from the open-range days of Johnson's grandfather, Sam Ealy Johnson, to ranching and farming of more recent times.

The LBJ Ranch, on the north bank of the Pedernales River and maintained by the National Park Service, contains the rambling ranch house that became the Texas White House, the reconstructed LBJ birthplace, the one-room Junction School attended by the president, and the family cemetery where the president is buried. South of the river, the Lyndon B. Johnson State Historical Park contains the visitor center that serves both parks. You should go to the State Park for National Park Service operated LBJ Ranch bus tours.

JOHNSON CITY UNIT

LBJ Boyhood Home

Lyndon Johnson's family moved from Stonewall, Texas, to the home in Johnson City at 9th and G Street two weeks after his fifth birthday in September 1913. For most of the next twenty-four years, this was their home.

The wood-frame one-story house built in 1901 is roughly cross-shaped in plan, with porches filling in the crosses' arms. The entrance to the house from the east front porch accesses the parlor and a small office. A double-face fireplace opens into the parlor and dining room. The "west wing" of the house (to the left of the central parlor, dining room, and kitchen) contains a small office, the girls' bedroom for LBJ's three sisters (Rebekah, Josefa, and Lucia) and a large sleeping porch at the northwest corner of the house. In the house's "east wing" are the parent's bedroom, the bedroom shared by LBJ with his brother, Sam Houston Johnson, a tub room, and a small porch.

The house's exterior of white-painted flush boards has a Victorian spirit with spindle trim boards at the west front porch and distinctive serrated trim board on the ridge of the gable roofs. A hint of Colonial Revival is seen in partial returns at the gable-end walls. The roofs intersect at a central chimney.

Lyndon B. Johnson restored boyhood home.

During the presidential years, the home was used as a community center and public tours were offered. In December 1969, Congress designated this home as part of Lyndon B. Johnson National Historic Site. The National Park Service has restored and furnished the home to its appearance during the mid-1920s, the teenage years of Lyndon B. Johnson.

Johnson Settlement

Soon after President Johnson retired from office, the National Park Service, with funds donated by the former president, purchased the Johnson Settlement area. Four historic nineteenth-century structures were still standing. Besides the two-room dogtrot log cabin built in the late 1850s by Samuel Ealy Johnson Sr., Lyndon's grandfather, they included a stone barn and cooler house.

You can linger in the Settlement's restored structures arranged around a pasture, usually with a few longhorns on display, to recall the early days of Texas cattle ranching. A chuck wagon near the log house is used for demonstrations of range-style cooking by cowboys in Stetson hats and leather chaps.

LBJ RANCH UNIT
Texas White House

The LBJ Ranch House is an imposing two-story structure facing the Pedernales River. The house was purchased by LBJ from a Johnson relative in 1951, and during the Johnson Administration it served as the Texas White House. Biographers of the president dwell on the significance of the ranch house in his securing a place of prestige and status that reflected his success and rootedness in the Pedernales Valley. The ranch also provided Johnson with a place to "recharge his batteries," as Lady Bird Johnson became fond of saying. In 1972, the Johnsons donated the Texas White House to the National Park Service and the American people. The park is part of Mrs. Johnson's legacy and represents her contribution to perpetrating the Texas White House as a living landscape. There is a guided bus tour of the LBJ Ranch; the ranch house is not accessible to the public.

The house's original section of native limestone fieldstone built in 1894 by a German immigrant, William "Polecat" Meier, saw successive additions and renovations throughout the years. Even after many additions and renovations, this stone element remains the house's defining element.

The Meiers added the clapboard-sided, wood-framed north wing about 1900, making the property one of the most impressive in the region. The main central portion of the house was added in 1909 after purchase of the property by the president's aunt and uncle, Frank and Clarence Martin. In 1912, the Martins enlarged the house, adding a two-story frame wing with a columned entrance connected to the stone portion by a front porch and central rooms. The addition of a music room and a parlor more than doubled the floor space in the home. The great fireplace and raised hearth that fronted it gave the front room a type of grandeur that was unparalleled in the typically more modest homes along the Pedernales River. Now an impressive mansion, the house became the center of family activities on the Pedernales. This was the place where LBJ spent his childhood summers and where he brought his bride, Claudia "Lady Bird" Taylor Johnson, to meet the Johnson family.

The Johnsons bought the home from Lyndon's aunt in 1951. The house needed considerable structural work and refurbishing, and the Johnsons made a number of additions, most notably the master bedrooms and the office wing. To the north of the house is a collection of outbuildings, a hangar, and an airstrip.

The National Park Service comments that the LBJ Ranch House provided "[Johnson] with a place to rest and clear his head; the ranch symbolized Johnson's aspirations and became the place he used to hone his political image." This is the Texas White House that you see today, a retreat from the pressures of Washington, where the president could host a steady stream of world leaders, political friends, and acquaintances while returning to his roots in the Pedernales Valley.

LBJ Reconstructed Birthplace

The LBJ birthplace home is a reconstruction of the original house torn down in the 1940s. Guided by the President with his interpretation and using photographs and family recollections, architect J. Roy White of Austin, Texas, designed the house in 1964 to follow the same architectural style as the original house, built in 1889 by the president's grandfather, Sam Ealy Johnson Sr.

Although on the original site, what you see now is considered a much nicer rendition; compare it to the 1897 photo hanging on the front wall of the barn behind the house. Planning of the reconstruction followed the original board-and-batten construction of the one-story house and included the central "dogtrot" hallway to provide cross-ventilation in hot weather. The conveniences of a modern kitchen and bathroom, running water, and electricity were added. Some salvaged pieces of the limestone fireplace and portions of the lumber were used in the reconstruction.

The house was used between 1964 and 1966 as a guest cottage for overflow company from the Texas White House. Furnishings represent antiques donated by family and special friends of the Johnsons. The president delighted in telling visitors that the kitchen had the only original piece of furniture—a rawhide bottom chair with a hole in the seat. Mrs. Johnson loaned the park her high chair in the kitchen. Etched on the back is "Lady Bird," the nickname given to Claudia Alta Taylor at age two.

Junction School

The Junction School was built in 1910 to serve as a school and church, serving the area for more than thirty-seven years. The restored wood-frame building, with brightly painted blue pressed-metal exterior walls, was a typical one-room schoolhouse. You can see the wood stove in a sand box in the center of the school, the only source of heat. Two kerosene lamps suspended from the ceiling at opposite ends of the room provided light. The teacher's desk and chair were in front of the classroom. A small brass bell on the teacher's desk summoned the students, who sat at double desks that had wooden tops with holes for the glass inkwells. The desks were arranged in rows facing the teacher's desk; the boys in one row and the girls in another.

Junction school was a short walk from home for the precocious four-year-old, and Johnson only attended the school for several months in 1912 since the school closed early due to a whooping cough epidemic. This was his first school, although young Lyndon tagged along with other children before he entered the school. He was reported as a favorite of teacher "Miss Katée" Deadrich who let him sit on her lap during reading time. His family moved to Johnson City by the start of the next school year, and in 1924, he graduated from high school in Johnson City. In the spring of 1947, the Junction School became part of the Stonewall Consolidated School District. This move closed the Junction School, and the students attended the nearby Stonewall School instead. In 1972, the National Park Foundation purchased the land to become part of the Lyndon B. Johnson National Historical Park. The President connected his attachment to the Junction School and quality public education for all children by signing the Elementary and Secondary Education Act on April 11, 1965, at a picnic table on the lawn of the Junction School, with Miss Katie Deadrich (his first teacher) at his side.

SAN ANTONIO MISSIONS

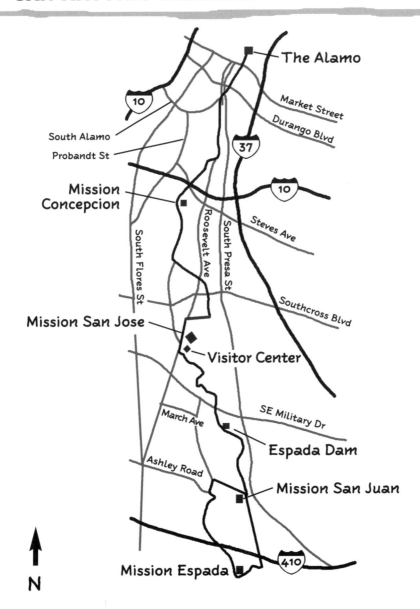

The Alamo

Market Street

Durango Blvd

South Alamo

Probandt St

10

37

Mission Concepcion

10

Steves Ave

Roosevelt Ave

South Presa St

South Flores St

Southcross Blvd

Mission San Jose

Visitor Center

SE Military Dr

March Ave

Espada Dam

Ashley Road

Mission San Juan

410

N

Mission Espada

4

San Antonio Missions
National Historical Park

San Antonio, Bexar County, Texas
www.nps.gov/saan

Start your tour of the Missions from the visitor center in downtown San Antonio, across the street from the Alamo, or from the visitor center adjacent to Mission San José. The four missions of San Antonio Missions National Historic Park are all located in south San Antonio. The Alamo is operated separately by the Daughters of the Texas Republic. With a tour brochure and map, brown-and-white Mission signs guide you on an all-day tour by car to all sites.

> "The missions [of San Antonio] evoke distinctive feelings for visitor and local resident alike. For the parishioners, the complexes are as much a part of their daily lives as their homes, their families or their jobs; they are a part of the tradition and continuity of their lives. For the visitors from nearby places, the structures are surviving reminders of that mysterious and romantic part of their Texas past, the days of the Spanish Empire. For all who travel to them, the sense of age, of mass, of substance and permanence, of the presence of the past unchanged, is profoundly felt."
>
> —Marlys Bush Thurber, *The Missions of San Antonio*, National Park Service

Close to the center of metropolitan San Antonio and connected by the Mission Trail leading from downtown are four Spanish frontier missions. Each mission complex is distinctive for its church as well as its interpretation by the National Park Service. The park sites maintained by agreement between the Archdiocese of San Antonio and the National Park Service provide visitors a special connection to the past.

San Antonio Missions National Historical Park preserves and interprets the missions as part of the heritage of Spanish colonization that stretched across the Southwest in the seventeenth, eighteenth, and nineteenth centuries. The missions included in the park are the active parish churches of Concepción, San José, San Juan, and Espada, established in the early 1700s. The park covers about 819 acres and was established in 1978. It contains the four missions, as well as Ranchos de las Cabras (in Wilson County), and other cultural and national areas.

Three miles south of downtown San Antonio, Mission Nuestra Señora de la Concepción de Acuña sits back from the road in a quiet,

Mission Concepción.

leafy residential area with an acre of lawn. The twin towers and pedimented main entry are good examples of the proportions of Colonial Baroque style. The most intact of the missions and claimed to be the oldest unrestored church in the United States, Concepción is a National Historic Landmark.

Mission San José y San Miguel de Aguayo, the largest and most impressive, and best preserved of the San Antonio's five missions, was founded in 1720. Identified by the single bell tower and wide façade, the elaborate Spanish Baroque *(Churrigueresque)* carvings at the entrance, attributed as "the finest Spanish Colonial façade in the United States" (Hugh Morrison, *Early American*

TEXAS

214

Mission San José.

Architecture, 1952), and rose window alone are worth the visit. The museum compound was reconstructed during the 1930s by the Works Progress Administration after the structure fell prey to vandalism and neglect in the nineteenth century.

Mission San Juan Capistrano has a smaller-scale church with several buildings, some ruined, with most of the walled compound visible. The mission is in a pastoral setting and is rather humble and muted in appearance. However, the charm of the mission is its simplicity, created by its buttressed church walls and distinctive silhouette, especially the simple and stark two-tiered pierced bell tower (*espadaña*). A quarter mile nature trail across from the entrance gate to the mission compound gives the visitor the opportunity to view the river and vegetation reminiscent of the early colonial landscape.

Mission San Francisco de la Espada is the southernmost church on the Mission Trail, surrounded by woodland in a peaceful rural setting, though just south of busy I-410. This is the oldest mission in Texas, originally situated by the Neches River in 1690. It was moved to its present location in 1731. The small church is distinctive for its Moorish-arched main entry and two-tiered pierced bell tower. The foundation of a larger church that was started in the 1760s but curtailed due to dwindling Indian population is seen near the mission church. Nearby is the Espada

Aqueduct, in use since 1740 and protected as a National Historic Landmark.

The missions flourished between 1745 and 1775. They were secularized in 1794 and completed in 1824. Increased hostility from Apaches and Comanches, coupled with military activity in the area, weakened them, and they gradually fell into ruin. Disease and absorption into the Hispanic population reduced the surrounding Indian population, accelerating the missions' decline. The mission era was over by 1824; farmers, soldiers, and squatters claimed their residences until well into the twentieth century. Neglect, vandalism, and war reduced some of the missions to ruins; glorious ornate polychrome exterior and interior decorations faded to ghost-like images.

Travelers of the nineteenth century poignantly described the lost grandeur of the missions. In 1857, Frederick Law Olmsted, in

Left: Mission Espada.
Below: Mission San Juan.

A Journey Through Texas, described them as "in different stages of decay, but they are all ruins, beyond any connection with the past—weird remains of the silent past."

Twenty years later, poet Spofford Harriet Prescott saw that "every one of these missions is now a ruin; the grass grows on so much of the roof that is left, the mesquite starts up in the long cloisters where the fathers used to pace, the cactus sprouts and blossoms in the crannies in the wall, the wild thyme hangs in bunches there, and sweetens all the lonesome summer air." Prescott poetically soared with descriptions of the churches: "Nothing can describe the solitary grandeur and beauty of Concepción, and the marvelous piece of color it makes . . . a vague pathos hangs over its broken arches and disused cells. . . . San José is both of finer design and workmanship . . . and more interesting La Espada towering above the dark foliage, a melancholy haunt of poetry and dreams."

At the turn of the previous century, church and civic leaders took on the task of stabilizing and restoring the mission ruins. In 1981, reflecting on his work as architect for the Preservation of the Missions, O'Neill Ford recalled:

> When I came to San Antonio in 1924, I was taken to see the "Mission Ruins," and indeed, that is precisely what one found at Espada, San Juan, and San José. . . . Concepción Mission was beautiful, firm, and scarcely touched by time and abuse, though it had suffered the same fate as the other missions by the barbarians who had carved their initials as high as their hands could reach. Very few San Antonians had any serious interest in the stark piles of rubble, and in general, it was assumed they would soon disappear or become stone quarries for well linings and other structures.

In 1928, the dramatic collapse of the San José church tower, which spared the ornate façade and famous rose window, initiated plans by the diocese for a comprehensive restoration of San Antonio's missions. Ironically, the efforts by the Conservation Society for the Archdiocese of San Antonio was stalled by the 1929 stock market crash, only to be infused with money and personnel by depression-era work-relief programs. Work on the San José Mission's reconstruction progressed in the 1930s through the combined efforts of the San Antonio Conservation Society, the Roman Catholic Church, Bexar County, and the Works Progress Administration (WPA). The real awakening of the mission's importance to Texas and national history gained momentum in the 1950s and 1960s with the potential role for tourism in San Antonio. The National Park Service was involved with San José from the 1930s during restoration as consultants. After 1941 and the designation of San José as a National Historic Site, annual visits were carried out to aid in the ongoing conservation of the site. Establishment of the San Antonio Missions National Historical Park in 1978 began a public-private partnership for the preservation and interpretation of the missions that continues today.

The Franciscan
♦ —————— Missions —————— ♦
of New Spain

The San Antonio missions' layout originated with Benedictine ideas of a monastery and adapted to meet circumstances of the sixteenth-century frontier for pacification and conversion of the indigenous people. Between 1730 and 1760, the Franciscans modified the original sixteenth-century schemes. The simple plan of the mission core complex—a church and adjoining cloister and central *patio* surrounded by a rectangle of buildings, combined with a village for the Indians laid out around a central square—was transformed into fortified villages to ward off constant threats of Apache and Comanche raids. Stone walls up to eight feet high and three feet thick surrounded a rectangular village, with a church and priest's quarters (*convento*) in one area. Indians and several soldiers with their families who lived at the mission had rooms inside the compound abutting the walls.

The first concern in establishing a mission was water, thus the location close to the San Antonio River. To assure a steady flow of water for the mission and for the irrigation of fields, a dam was built across the river and a ditch (*acequia*) dug to divert water. The Espada Dam and Aqueduct over the Piedras Creek, the only aqueduct still in use from the Spanish Colonial period in the United States, was completed in 1745 and is still functioning today.

The Texas missions were constructed in a mixture of styles derived from Spain through Mexico—colorful Moorish designs, Romanesque forms, and Gothic arches—that would evolve in New Spain into the Spanish Colonial–style churches. Rexford Newcomb, in *Spanish Colonial Architecture in the United States* (1937), concluded that "the charm of the mission churches may in measure be said to consist of a certain naïve simplicity and a rugged straight-forwardness that is as interesting as it is rare."

The following terms may help visitors understand the layouts of the missions:

Church

The church is the central place of worship, generally configured as a cross in plan. In front of the church was a courtyard *(atrio)* enclosed by a low wall. Decorative framing surrounded the main entry (portal) to the church. Above the portal was a window, sometimes round (oculus, or eye), a Christian symbol for the eye of God opening to the orb of the heavens. A choir loft and a vestibule under the loft *(sotocorro)* were placed inside the main entry.

The central space for worship was the long longitudinal space (nave) where the congregation kneeled or stood for services. Sometimes the plan included a transept, a transverse portion that crossed the nave at a right angle under a dome. The sanctuary at the end of the nave, opposite from the entry and separated from the congregation, contained the altar, altar table, side altar, altars, and altar screen *(reredo* or *retablo)* that served as the backdrop for the celebration of the Mass. A sacristy is a room attached to the sanctuary for priests' robing and preparation for services, as well as storage of vestments, books, and sacred vessels. An apse could extend beyond the sanctuary and contain the main altar and *reredo.*

Convento

Arched passageways *(corredores)* enclosed spaces around one or more patios (or garths) containing clergy's housing and living quarters, working quarters, a dining hall for clergy (refectory), a guest room for visiting clergy (hospice, or *hospederia)*, an infirmary for sick clergy offices and work areas *(oficinas)* for the clergy, and a kitchen *(cocina)*. Some missions with a second *patio* adjoining the *convento* could include additional work-rooms and shops. A cemetery *(camposanto)* enclosed by walls was sometimes located at the side of the church. Also many of the missionaries, community leaders and family members were buried in the church, either close to the altar or in the side chapels.

The missions are described in sequence traveling south from downtown San Antonio along the Mission Trail. Bring your camera and enjoy a leisurely day.

MISSION NUESTRA SEÑORA DE LA CONCEPCIÓN DE ACUÑA

Mission Concepción was named in honor of Our Lady of the Immaculate Conception and Juan de Acuña, the Marqués de Casafuerte and Viceroy of New Spain (Mexico) when the mission was transferred to the San Antonio River area in 1731 and completed in 1755.

This handsome example of Colonial Baroque architecture was started in 1740 and appears very much as it did more than two centuries ago. Mission Concepción has the oldest unreconstructed church and *convento* in the Southwest. In its heyday, colorful geometric designs covered its surface, but the patterns have long since faded or worn away. The walls, workshops, and living quarters at Mission Concepción have long been torn down and removed. Don't be discouraged by the somber gray walls. What is left is well worth your visit to see colorful Moorish design influences and intricate Renaissance details complementing Romanesque forms and gothic arches.

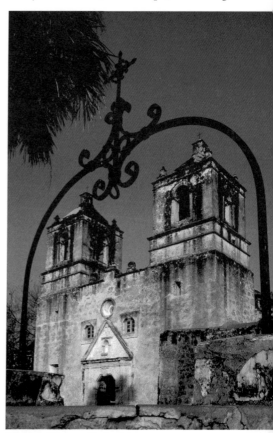

Despite abandonment, deface-ment, and partial destruction, the church remained structurally intact, due to its forty-five-inch-thick load-bearing wall construction of dressed stone on both sides, filled with stone rubble and adobe.

The cruciform-plan church has twin belfry towers, capped by a pyramidal roof and finials, a barrel-vaulted roof, and a dome at the cross-ing. The church is ninety-three feet long from apse to portal, fifty-three feet wide at the transepts, and the dome rises to an interior height of forty-four feet. North and east walls were made windowless for defensive purposes. The front elevation is divided into three bays; ornately

Mission Concepción bell tower.

carved stone columns supporting a steep triangular pediment frame a main entrance door in the central bay. The original effect was much different than you see today. The entire façade was plastered and frescoed with yellow and orange squares filled with red and blue quatrefoils and crosses, painted quoins marked the corners, and painted columns flanked each opening in the bell towers.

The six-room *convento* with attached *corredor*, measuring forty-two feet by eighty-six feet in outside dimensions, is L-shaped in plan. The arcaded *corredor* extends along the west wall of the church and is reinforced by buttresses. A barrel-vaulted room in the *convento* still bears polychrome fresco decorations on its walls and ceiling.

The rich painted decorations are some of the earliest surviving examples of mission decorative arts in the Southwest. An international effort in 1988 restored the frescoes and paintings in the library. New color was brought to the centuries-old frescoes by reattaching delaminated plaster on the wall surfaces and removing damaging salts that had turned the decorative surfaces powdery.

Mission Concepción main entrance.

MISSION SAN JOSÉ Y SAN MIGUEL DE AGUAYO

The mission named for Saint Joseph and the Marqués de San Miguel de Aguayo, the governor of Texas, and Coahula was considered the most important and was a veritable fortress. The church is referred to as the Queen of Missions. It is the most impressive of the San Antonio missions and an extraordinary example of

Mission San José stone carving at side entrance.

Colonial Baroque architecture. Conceived on a grand scale and built between 1768 and 1782 at the height of the Baroque period in Mexico, the decorative style is on a par with the finest churches of the time in the larger cities of Mexico.

Mission San José served as the headquarters of the father president of the Zacatean missions of Texas. At the height of the mission's influence in 1778, Father Juan Antonio Morfi wrote, "It is, in truth, the first mission in America . . . in point of beauty, plan and strength . . . there is not a presidio along the entire frontier line that can compare with it." Father Morfi praised the church, still under construction, for its size, good taste, and beauty, adding that "no one could have imagined there were such good artists in so desolate a place."

Construction on the new church began in 1768. The original plan for the new church laid out a long nave, two bell towers, and a transept. Modified during construction, the completed church was shorter and had only one bell tower. Construction on the second was stopped at the church's roofline, and a gun platform was built on top. The transept was never built, and the sacristy with its unique roof and three domes was moved and enlarged on the site of the proposed transept. The church and sacristy were completed in 1782.

Between 1868 and 1872, the dome and vaulted roof collapsed into the church. The circular stairway against the south bell tower collapsed in 1928. Both were rebuilt in the same year. The mission had fallen into disrepair and partial ruin over the years through upheavals of secularization, changes in national allegiance, structural collapses, and vandalism. The San Antonio Conservation Society and

Mission San José rose window.

the federal government, among others, undertook to restore portions of the mission in the 1920s and 1930s. Architect Harvey P. Smith began a major reconstruction of the mission from 1929 to 1935. So that the mission would resemble its post-1760 appearance, the federally assisted work included rebuilding the north wall, vault, and dome of the church; reconstructing the granary's vaulted roof; and building replica Indian quarters and compound walls on their old foundations. The church was rededicated in 1937; in 1941, Mission San José was declared a State Historic Site, and later that same year, a National Historic Site.

Approach the entrance gate at the southwest corner of the surrounding stone wall, one of four gateways all reconstructed during the 1930s. The gate structures are built of random rubble masonry, spanned by segmental stone arches, with double wooden gates (restored in the 1970s) that open into the compound and can be barred shut. Each gateway has *vigas* projecting inward towards the compound that support a boardwalk along the parapet.

Fragment of San José church vibrant plaster decoration.

Enter the approximately five-hundred-by-six-hundred-foot mission compound, lined on three sides by eighty-four flat-roofed apartments for Christianized Indians and sweep your eyes around the enclosure. A restored vaulted and buttressed granary stands in the northwest corner; a prefecture and quarters for the one or two soldiers and their families garrisoned there from the nearby presidio comprise the fourth wall. In the northeast corner of the compound is the church and missionaries quarters (*convento*) and, in the foreground, the *convento* gardens.

The church, approximately thirty-three by one hundred feet, is rectangular in plan. The façade, sixty-two feet wide, sparkles with decorative detailing. The single bell tower rises to a height of more than seventy-five feet. Originally, the entire façade of dressed limestone walls with corner quoins was plastered and frescoed to resemble bright tiles. A small sample of the geometric patterns can be seen near the lower right corner of the tower. The towers, the dome, and circular choir stairway collapsed at least once, and all were rebuilt to what may be seen today.

Mission San José church main entrance.

It is the main entrance with its richness of Spanish Baroque ornament, contrasted with the simple façade wall, that will draw your attention. The elaborateness of carved stone details—pilasters, scrollwork, shells, flowers and foliage, niches, and statues, set around the entry doors, with a balcony at an oval window, topped by a cross—contribute to the mission worthy of the name "Queen of Missions." The richly carved doors, reproduced in 1937 by Peter Mansbendel using historic stereoscopic images, replaced those removed in the 1890s. Above the entrance, statues of St. Dominic and St. Francis of Assisi flank likenesses of the mission's patron saint, St. Joseph. Smaller statues of St. Joachim and St. Anne flanking the entrance were restored in the 1940s.

Today, an unornamented church interior of plastered, off-white walls with simple painted decoration soars to a groined barrel roof, taller than the church's width. Over the transept location is an octagon drum, smoothed to a circle on the interior; the sixty-foot-high hemispherical dome rests on pendentives. Southern light entering through windows high in the walls and the sound of the drum is constant throughout the day. An ornately carved doorway on the south wall leads to the triple-domed sacristy with carved columns.

Around the church's tower corner is the cylindrical tower leading to the choir loft and bell tower; inside is a remarkable circular stairway of solid local oak, which swings on a central pivot. Further along the walk to the *convento*, pause to admire the rose window in the sacristy wall. A grillwork-covered window surrounded by ornately stone-carved scrolls and foliage, *La Ventana de Rosa*

Interior of San José church.

(the rose window) has been the object of both legend and admiration. One local legend is that the mason's ardor for a woman named Rosa gave her the honor of the "Rose Window" being named after her.

The ornamented, arched sacristy doorway opening into the convento corridor contains a cedar-paneled door. Refinished and installed in 1953, it is the original door and may be one of very few items of wood that has survived from the colonial period.

The *convento* is intriguing, as time has removed elements of the building to reveal the remains of the two-story structure. The upper story housed missionaries while the lower floor included various storerooms, workrooms, and offices. The ruins show the segmental, round, and lancet arches built on load-bearing masonry walls of rubble limestone and sandstone set with lime mortar. The 70-by-136-foot quarters for the Franciscan missionaries were built as a series of interconnected rooms opening to a ground-floor cloister and second-floor *corredor*. The *convento* garden, due south of the *convento*, is outlined by a roughly coursed three-foot-high stone wall.

During the reconstruction of the mission in the 1920s and 1930s, the *convento* was not rebuilt. In the 1850s, Benedictine monks from Latrobe, Pennsylvania, purchased the mission complex from the diocese of San Antonio to develop it as a school for boys. Much of the original Romanesque work was replaced by incongruous Gothic arches before the American Civil War intervened and the property reverted to the diocese. In deference to the changes from the original Spanish Colonial structure, restoration was limited to stabilization.

The granary *(troje)* in the northeast corner of the enclosed compound was the first building at Mission San José to be restored in the 1920s. Built to store grain or produce, the building is identified by its rubble-stone walls and flying buttresses. Approximately 110 by 35 feet in plan, masonry load-bearing walls support a barrel vault over a flagstone floor.

The Indian quarters are replicas of the eighteen-foot-wide units, built with load-bearing limestone walls and flat roofs lining the compound walls. Wood lintels span all of the doors and window openings facing the mission plaza. The reconstructed doors of native mesquite wood are hung on replicas of iron hinges found during excavations in the 1930s. Various rooms have been adapted for use as concessions, rest areas, restrooms, and storage.

MISSION SAN JUAN CAPISTRANO

The third of the missions south from San Antonio on the Mission Trail, Mission San Juan Capistrano is charming for the simplicity of its architecture in a pastoral setting. The array of gray stone buildings around a grassy plaza defined by a low stone wall is a puzzle of parts. The active parish church is identified by the pierced bell tower and buttressed walls; to the left is the

Mission San Juan Capistrano bell tower.

restored *convento*, which serves as the visitor center and small museum; on the right are the granary and residences. Ruins of the compound walls and larger church with its unusual octagonal sacristy, Indian quarters, and houses built from the wall rubble define the mission complex.

Originally founded in 1716 in eastern Texas, Mission San Juan was transferred in 1731 to its present location. In 1756, the stone church, a friary, and a granary were completed. By the mid-1700s, San Juan was a self-sustaining community with a trade surplus that helped its settlers survive epidemics and Indian attacks for years. A larger church was begun but was abandoned when half complete, the result of decline in the Indian population. At the time of final secularization of the mission in 1824, an inventory listed the incomplete church, the present chapel, *convento*, and fifteen stone houses.

Charles Mattoon Brooks, an architect visiting the mission in 1936 observed the mission's deterioration. He saw the church "is appallingly disintegrated" and the *convento* "crumbling."

The present church, with arched and buttressed walls and the bell tower facing the plaza, was constructed partially over the foundations of a granary that was added to the *convento* sometime between 1772 and 1786. The five

Interior of San Juan church.

stone buttresses along the church's east wall were added in 1968 to stabilize the structure.

The church and sacristy is rectangular in plan, with overall exterior dimensions of 20 by 110 feet; the sacristy is a room measuring fifteen feet square on the interior. The church's plan is unusual for the primary and secondary entrances placed in the east wall of the nave. Construction is random rubble masonry. The interior is a simple space, restored in the 1960s. Lacking the rich Baroque decorative work of Mission San José, the flat ceiling of exposed beams and *latillas* rises above the white-painted walls that were once covered with colorful frescoes including depictions of musicians playing instruments.

The *convento*, also extensively reconstructed in the 1960s, is the remnant of a compound that housed the Franciscans, workrooms, and storage rooms. The building now serves as mission visitor contact station and museum. Structures in the northwest corner of the compound are built on the foundations and walls of Indian quarters and nineteenth-century walls. The gable-ended stone-masonry structures were reconstructed in the 1960s.

Mission Concepción.

MISSION SAN FRANCISCO DE LA ESPADA
Mission Complex

The southernmost of the San Antonio missions, Mission San Francisco de la Espada was heavily fortified to ward off frequent Apache and Comanche raids. At this distance from downtown San Antonio, you have a sense of its remoteness. Notable features of this charming complex are the remaining stone compound walls, the church with a distinctive Moorish-arched entrance and bell tower, the *convento* (closed for use as a refectory), the Indian quarters, and the bastion at the southeast corner.

Founded in 1690 as San Francisco de los Tejas near present-day Weches, this was the first mission in Texas. In 1731, the mission was transferred to the San Antonio River area and renamed Mission San Francisco la Espada. A *convento* was built at Espada in 1745. The church was completed in 1756. A more impressive stone church started in 1762 was never completed. After the mission was secularized in 1824 and gradually fell into ruins, it was returned to usage in 1858 with the arrival of a young French priest named Francois Bouchu, who arrived to find the mission in ruins; he worked with his own hands to rebuild the church until his death in 1909. Acknowledged as the church's rescuer, his tireless efforts established Espada as a parish church.

The modest scale of today's Espada church is due to its construction in 1740 as the sacristy for what was to be the final church at Espada. There is a reported episode of an early granary converted to a new church around 1775 that was torn down because it threatened to collapse and was never completed. Foundation ruins southeast of the stone well in the courtyard suggest the impressive size of the planned church. The original sacristy-church continued in use throughout the colonial period. The sacristy's modest size was expanded to today's cruciform plan, approximately twenty-five by sixty-five feet.

The entry façade is a simple rectangle unadorned with Baroque decoration, distinctive for its two-tiered three-bell tower (*espadaña*), recalling that of Mission San Juan. The shape of the unique Moorish entry arch has several explanations. One theory is that the order of stones at the top of the arch was reversed. Whether produced by error or not, it recalls a Moorish arch, a familiar element in Spanish architecture. To the left of the doorway is a wooden cross that legend claims was carried by the parishioners during a time of drought as they led a procession around the compound, praying for rain.

The flat-roofed structure of load-bearing sandstone walls is approximately seventeen feet high. The interior of the church is attractively simple. The width is pleasantly proportioned to the height of the exposed corbel-bracketed ceiling beams and

Mission Espada.

weathered wood-deck ceiling. Pairs of tall arched windows on the nave's sides flood the space with daylight. Along the side walls are pairs of wooden crosses marking the Stations of the Cross. Wrought-iron candelabras are placed high on the walls. Statues of *Jesus Nazareno* and *Our Lady of Solitude* flank the altar, and an image of Saint Francis from the late eighteenth century is above the altar. The interior flooring of quarry tile adds to the church's warm intimacy.

The *convento* compound extends from the church's south wall. The flat-roofed two-story building, reconstructed on the ruins of the original *convento* and mission-manufactured kitchen built from 1740–60, is recognized by its segmental arches, with soffits faced with brick, on the courtyard façade. The *convento* is used as a parish rectory and is closed to the public.

Other features of the compound are the ruins of a granary, Indian quarters, and the L-shaped bastion and adjoining rooms. The eighteen-foot-diameter bastion, possibly built in the early 1880s, faced towards open country to the south.

Espada Dam and Aqueduct

Installation of an *acequia* (irrigation) system for a reliable water source was a high priority in south-central Texas. The Franciscans adopted the system from Roman and Arab-inspired irrigation used in Spain. Water was important in Spanish Texas, and farmland was measured by areas that could be watered in one day, called *suertes*. In order to distribute water to the missions along the San Antonio River, Franciscan missionaries oversaw the construction of a system of five gravity-flow ditches, dams, and at least one aqueduct. It was a fifteen-mile network that irrigated approximately 3,500 acres of farmland *(labores)*. The Espada system is the best preserved of these *acequias*.

Mission Espada's *acequia* system is a remarkable feat of Spanish Colonial engineering that continues to carry water to the mission and neighboring farmlands. The Espada Dam on the San Antonio River can be seen from the parkway between Mission San Jose and Mission San Juan. Changed little from its construction around 1745, the dam is built of rubble limestone, later capped by Portland cement, and is eight feet high, five feet thick at the top, and 185 feet long. The Espada Dam is still in operation, although it plays a secondary role to the modern dam. Water from the old San Antonio River channel flows into the main water ditch *(acequia madre)* to irrigate Mission Espada's fields, and ultimately flows back into the river south of Mission Espada.

Espada Aqueduct, was built to carry water from the San Antonio River across a small creek. This astonishing structure was completed around 1745, and Espada Aqueduct still carries water over Piedras Creek to fields near the mission, just as it did more then two and a half centuries ago. It is the only functioning stone aqueduct from the Spanish Colonial period in the United States. Using a system of floodgates, the water master *(mayordomo)* controlled the volume of water sent through ditches to each field for irrigation and for other uses such as bathing, washing, and powering mill wheels.

The mission's rescue from ruins is a tribute to individuals, local preservation groups, and the federal government. The National Park Service continues its partnership with the Arch diocese of San Antonio and civic leaders to preserve and interpret this fascinating part of our country's history. Founded when Texas was in the northern reaches of New Spain (Mexico), the missions continue to serve as parish churches. The missions are open year round from 9:00 A.M. to 5:00 P.M., except New Year's day, Thanksgiving, and Christmas day. Enjoy the frequent festivals with lots of music, food, and color, sponsored by the local parishes. Religious festivities may include holiday celebrations. After Christmas, either the last week of December or the first week in January, a morality play, Los Pastores, is enacted at Mission San José in the evening, in November, the park's friends group, Los Compradres, sponsors Artesanos del Pueblo, a week-end of arts and crafts demonstrations and sales. Remember also that the missions are fragile resources and places of worship.

INDEX

233

INDEX